D1289484

Vermonters

Vermonters

ORAL HISTORIES FROM DOWN COUNTRY TO THE NORTHEAST KINGDOM

Ron Strickland

Chronicle Books • San Francisco

Copyright © 1986 by Ron Strickland. All
rights reserved. No part of this book may be
reproduced in any form without written per-
mission from the publisher.

Printed in Japan

Library of Congress
Cataloging-in-Publication Data

Strickland, Ron.
    Vermonters: Oral Histories from Down
Country to the Northeast Kingdom.

    Includes index.
    1. Vermont—Social life and customs.
2. Vermont—Biography.   I. Title.
F54.S78   1986   974.3   86-14738
ISBN 0-87701-394-2 (pbk.)

Editing: Deborah Stone
Book and cover design: Naomi Schiff
Composition: TBH/Typecast, Inc.

Photo credits:
All nonhistorical photographs by the author,
except the following:
Coos County Democrat, Lancaster, N.H.; p. 87
Daniels, Peggy Pearl: pp. 38, 126
Courtesy Governor Kunin: p. 70
Russell, Glenn: p. 147
Rutland Herald, Rutland, Vermont, p. 9
Stevens, Harry R.: p. 14

Front Cover
  Guy Osgood (center) and his father (left)
Back Cover
  Charles Ross at the state capital

10 9 8 7 6 5 4 3 2 1

Chronicle Books
One Hallidie Plaza
San Francisco, CA 94102

Contents

➤➤➤➤➤➤➤➤➤➤➤➤➤➤➤➤➤➤➤➤⊗◄◄◄◄◄◄◄◄◄◄◄◄◄◄◄◄◄◄◄◄◄

Introduction

➤➤➤➤➤➤➤➤➤➤➤➤➤➤➤➤➤ ⊛ ◀◀◀◀◀◀◀◀◀◀◀◀◀◀◀◀◀◀◀◀◀

THE NAME *Vermont* stirs immediate reactions in people all across America. For most, the state evokes Currier and Ives images of covered bridges; steepled nineteenth-century towns; radiant autumn colors; dazzling winter landscapes; serpentine country roads; and soothing, pastoral calm. The Vermonters themselves, we know, have a penchant for certain enduring icons of American life—the direct democracy of the town meeting; the independent-mindedness of the Green Mountain Boys; and the laconic canniness of the legendary farmer who, generation after generation, directs lost flatlanders into backroad oblivion.

The amazing thing, at the end of the twentieth century, is that this quaint picture of Vermont still contains so much truth. Vermont, of course, has evolved constantly. The pioneer era of the late eighteenth century has given way to the sheep culture of pre–Civil War days followed in turn by the great Western exodus; the dairying period, which still exists in places; the ongoing changes in forestry technology; the alarms over acid rain; and the the increasing gentrification and touristification of much of the state.

One of the most popular books west of the Connecticut River and east of "York state" recently was *Real Vermonters Don't Milk Goats*. It asks the humorous question, "How do you recognize a real Vermonter?" In my Vermont travels, I asked instead, "Who most influenced your life and how did that inspiration show itself in your work?"

In researching my earlier book, *River Pigs and Cayuses: Oral Histories from the Pacific Northwest*, I noticed that many people held on to the influence of early role models. Inspirational figures—whether they be family members, friends, co-workers, neighbors, or unmet but greatly admired personages—immeasurably enrich our lives. With such people figuratively or physically in our lives, we do not have to reinvent the wheel. We are

1

buoyed up by a conviction that the impossible has been achieved and that we too can succeed.

I have been fortunate to have had many heroes. In the 1970s, when I was pioneering the Pacific Northwest Trail between the Continental Divide and the Pacific Ocean, I often thought of fellow New Englander Benton MacKaye's labors to create the Appalachian Trail during the 1920s. And the appreciation of nature in my book *Going the Distance: The Pacific Northwest Trail* owes a direct debt to the late Henry Beston and Sigurd Olson. Today I still turn to their writings for inspiration and solace.

Heroes become ours for the asking.

Assembled in these pages are the most memorable Vermonters I could find to represent their small, spirited state. In the last census, Vermont had the third smallest population among the fifty states. Of its half million people, 66.2 percent lived in communities of twenty-five hundred inhabitants or less, making Vermont the most rural American state. Although this may be just what we would expect of that Currier and Ives countryside of legend, the figures are deceptive. Even back in the sixties, a quarter of Vermont's population had been born elsewhere. And don't forget about summer's great influx of part-time Vermonters, a number not reflected in any census.

To be fully accepted in Vermont, the tradition goes, you must be at least a third generation Vermonter. That notion has been much eroded by the large number of newcomers—including the present governor—from "down country" or "away."

I am one of those flatlanders myself: I visited Vermont while hiking with my family in the Green Mountains twenty-five years ago, for instance, and participated and later worked at the Experiment In International Living in Putney in 1964 and 1965. My occasional sojourns here were supplemented throughout the sixties by immersion in the books of Dorothy Canfield Fisher and Helen and Scott Nearing. I have always been an impressionable and romantic fellow and those literary heroes very early stamped the name *Vermont* on my heart.

Vermonters: Oral Histories from Down Country to the Northeast Kingdom is about change and about continuity. If Burlington's Socialist mayor Bernie Sanders symbolizes the former, then Chelsea's house-calling country doctor Brewster Martin symbolizes the latter. In true Vermont fashion, Dr. Martin does not consider himself a local man, even though he grew up only forty miles away in Pittsfield. "Although I was was born in Vermont," Dr. Martin says, "I'm not a native of this town. You're sort of reminded of that in subtle little ways. You move in and you have big ideas of how to improve and change it and the longer you live here the more you realize that they're right and you're wrong. 'Be not the first by whom the new are tried nor the last to set the old aside.' That's my grandmother. [*Laughter.*]

It's true. It really is. There are a lot of neat old things and traditions that are worth hanging onto."

I found my Vermonters the same way you would go about finding a good person to cut your timber or dowse a site for a new well. I asked around. One good storyteller often led to another. Once I even discussed my quest for heroes for half an hour on a St. Johnsbury radio station. There and everywhere I traveled the response was very satisfying: My search for the human thread of inspiration struck a responsive chord.

From the darkest, coldest heart of winter 1985 to the beginning of maple and mud season, I established a base in the Northeast Kingdom—so named by that archetypal Vermonter, the late governor and U.S. senator George Aiken—and scoured the state for representative stories.

Oh, I had my failures out on the frozen roads and in the snowy door-yards. There were times I was thrown into the uncomfortable role of the flatlander who asks the Yankee farmer if he has lived here all his life and gets the classic response: "Not yet." I remember one painful afternoon spent at a too-good-to-be-true country store and post office in Orange County. The storekeeper and his premises could have emerged through a time machine directly from the late nineteenth century. The harnesses, foods, tools, red-checkered hats, and folksy talk reminded me strongly of the country stores I knew as a boy just after World War II in Rhode Island. The place had that patina of age, use, and stale gossip which cannot be duplicated over on the tourist highways. But the proprietor was not talking. In desperation I kept buying things, hoping to draw him into conversation. First, I bought post cards. *Nope. Yup.* Then stamps. *Nope. Yup.* Doughnuts. *Nope. Yup.* After I bought some expensive cans of maple syrup, I called it quits. You cannot buy words or stories or parts of the soul.

The relationship of outsiders to the natives is always a complex one—and part of the fun. Bill Godfrey, eighty five, is one of my favorite Vermonters. A retired auctioneer and and sugarmaker, he is still an active undertaker on Blood Brook near Ely, not far north of Dartmouth College. In an accent thick enough to chop wood with, he laughed through the following story about some new neighbors he once had.

> People move in here and, of course, they think Vermonters are all green. When you get right down to it, they're the green ones. They try to tell you what to do, but the first thing you know *they're* out of business.
>
> Up above here some folks from California bought a second home. I owned a seventy-five-acre lot up beyond theirs to which I had a right-of-way. One day the woman and her husband came down. "I'm your new neighbor from California," she said. I says,

"You are?" And she said, "Yes. I've come down to see the man who has a right-of-way through our property." I said, "Well, you're lookin right at him."

She saw my big garden—I always have about an acre—and she asked if I had it every year. I said yes and she said, "Well, I'll show you how to make a garden next year. We're going to have a garden." I thought, Well, I've heard them folks talk before; it don't worry me any.

So the next year they plowed a piece out south of their house. I don't know what they planted in it, but I don't think they ever touched it. I went up there one day and the weeds were about four foot high; not a vegetable in sight.

They'd bought one of those rototillers that they claim never ball up. The weeds had wound right around that about the size of one of them old wooden nail kegs. She said, "Don't you want to take it down and try it?" I said, "No, I don't want to try it; I've got one I like better than that. Mine don't wind up so bad."

That was the last of their gardening. They moved away. But they'd come on here from California and they were going to show *us* how to do business.

A lot of these people come in here and try to tell ya how to do things and the first thing you know they're out on the limb.

People kept telling me that the true Vermonter is a dying breed. If accents are any indication, that's certainly true. The strongly regional pronounciation of a Bill Godfrey is missing in the Vermont school children I know.

In 1965, as a student counselor at Putney's Experiment In International Living, I supervised a group of visiting foreign students doing a survey of local views on whether to combine Putney's grammar school with that of neighboring towns. Way up those dirt roads, my wide-eyed, culture-shocked charges and I discovered ways of speaking that were direct links to colonial America. For years afterward, I wished that I could have stayed to get to know those irreplaceable Putneyites.

Now I have achieved that long ago wish to some small degree. In this book you will travel with me to sugar bushes, cemeteries, hill farms, schools, city halls, sawmills, fishing shanties, performance stages, general stores, and snowplow cabs. I am excited to share the Vermont I know with you.

I hope you will remember the Green Mountain State for its people. I certainly remember Bud Pearl's gloriously happy expression as he told me about his great-aunt. Or Doc La Bounty thinking about the big perch and trout lurking under his fishing shanty. Or Wilma Farman recalling the fun at her Squabble Hollow one-room schoolhouse. Or Chet Grimes, lovingly tending his huge horses, telling me about the great teamsters of his youth.

No more than the mentors and heroes who inspired them are these people likely to be memorialized in bronze, granite, or marble. They are, as my youngest storyteller Becky Bangs, who is twenty six, put it, "ordinary people doing extraordinary things."

Memory, experience, and the narrative urge are the raw materials novelists, poets, entertainers, and balladeers carve and burnish into rich gems of invention. I believe that at its best nothing can surpass the warmth and drama of a single voice speaking directly to us of the things that matter. The campfire flickers on the rapt faces. The radio reader charms and gladdens through the limpid pulses of the air. A pastor delivers a sermon full of passion and life. A parent invents a fable for the falling-asleep child. Our impersonal age cries out for this balm, the healing touch of words, the storyteller's art.

Lola Aiken

ADMINISTRATIVE ASSISTANT TO GOVERNOR AIKEN

Montpelier, Vermont
Born: "I always say that anybody who will tell their age will tell anything."

➤➤➤➤➤➤➤➤➤➤➤➤➤➤➤➤➤ ✪ ◄◄◄◄◄◄◄◄◄◄◄◄◄◄◄◄◄

AT THE END OF THE FISCAL YEAR June 30, 1967, Senator Aiken surprised everyone by marrying his long-time administrative assistant Lola Pierotti. He immediately took her off his payroll, though she continued to work full-time as office manager. Lola Pierotti Aiken says that she used to tell "the Governor" that he was the most interesting man she ever knew. "And he used to laugh about it, but it's true."

George Aiken, born in 1892, was governor of Vermont from 1937 to 1941 and U.S. senator for thirty-six years until 1974. He retired from the Senate at the age of eighty two and died on November 19, 1984. Although his Senate leadership was notable in numerous issues, from food stamps to Vietnam ("Just say we won and get out"), he was most effective in a purely nonlegislative way. He was that lucky man whose personal virtues and quirks become identified in the public mind with those of his homeplace. To many Aiken *was* Vermont.

In the Democratic sweep of 1936, he had been one of only four Republicans elected governor. In the late thirties, George Aiken was a nationally prominent critic of the "big government" New Deal; he made an abortive presidential bid in 1938. Yet he was not a doctrinaire party man. His Senate biographical sketch always described his occupation as farmer. He grew up on a remote southeast Vermont hill farm, was a Granger since 1907, operated a nursery business and wrote learnedly about wildflowers, and

worked throughout his political career to represent that increasingly obsolete class of small farmers from which he had sprung. His views were those
of an enlightened husbandman. He had a good Yankee blend of common
sense, thoughtfulness, humor, and closeness to the land. Politicians nowadays talk about a balanced budget, but when this old farmer talked about
it he backed up his words with a life of personal example. His political
virtues were those of Chapter XVI of Vermont's *Declaration of Rights:*

> That frequent recurrence to fundamental principles, and a firm
> adherence to justice, moderation, temperance, industry and frugal-
> ity, are absolutely necessary to preserve the blessings of liberty,
> and keep government free.

Note the characteristic Vermont inclusion of the word *frugality.*

Because George Aiken comes first in this book as my quintessential Vermonter, I want to preface Lola Aiken's reminiscence with a rather long
quotation from *Aiken: Senate Diary.* Written during his tumultuous last
three years as dean of the U.S. Senate, it speaks forcefully of a man whose
heart was in the right place.

Putney, Vermont

This is the first day of the New Year, 1972.

Up here on Putney Mountain five miles from town, eight inches
of new snow are piled upon a foot of old snow and crust, the tem-
perature a little below zero, but mostly sunshine and no wind.

Looking off to the east, we can see a twenty-mile stretch of the
New Hampshire hills east of the Connecticut River. Mount
Monadnock dominates the view, now that the leaves are off the
trees. On clear nights, the lights of New Hampshire homes blink
at us from the distance, while during late summer and early fall
evenings we look out from our vantage point of fourteen hundred
feet elevation in full sunshine over a sea of fog filling the Connecticut Valley.

Two hundred years ago this mountain was covered with virgin
forests, and just to think of the work, the courage, and endured
hardships of the early settlers cannot help but give one a mixed
feeling of pride and guilt. Pride that this land was cleared and this
country was built by those ancestors of ours who had the courage
and faith which prompted them to leave the oppression and
tyranny of their mother countries to face hostile elements in
America in order to be free. And a touch of guilt at the volume of

Governor and Mrs. Aiken

complaints we receive when the luxuries of modern living fail to arrive on time or the vacation trip to exotic countries has to be passed up for one reason or another.

New Year's Eve was cloudless, the moon was full, glistening on the snow so that one could almost read a newspaper out-of-doors through most of the night. The effect of full moonlight shining through the white birches with a background of pine and hemlock is indescribably beautiful, conveying the glory and Power of the Infinite in a manner never before heard from podium or pulpit.

I worked for the secretary of state of Vermont and knew Governor Aiken's secretary when he was governor. She asked if I would come to Washington. That's how I became his top secretary and then administrative assistant.

When I first went to work for him, I didn't like him because if I went in to tell him something and he was reading a paper, he would just go on reading. That annoyed the hell out of me. I discovered later he'd heard every word I said. It's a typical Vermont trait. They never let you know they're paying close attention to you. And yet they hear every word you say.

The Governor was a typical Vermonter in so many ways. If you tried to get a specific answer out of him, he'd say, "We'll see. Maybe." He never said yes or no.

They're very sharp, but you never know it. You underestimate them because thay always look like they're not with it. But they are.

The Governor had another trick. Somebody would ask him a question and he would reply to a completely different question. Later I would say, "Governor, you didn't answer the question." He'd say, "I know I didn't; I didn't want to answer that question."

So somebody would think, Well, he didn't hear what I said. He heard, but he didn't want to give an answer. They just assumed that he was losing his hearing or something.

I remember that a reporter for the Rutland Herald mentioned it one time. The publisher started to laugh and he said, "George Aiken's always been like that."

After you knew the Governor awhile, you began to get wise to him. Then you started looking at him from a different point of view and you realized he was an incredible person. Very soon I discovered he was a wonderful human being. Very understated. Very much himself.

I was administrative assistant when I married him on June 27, 1967 at the end of that fiscal year. He took me off the payroll on that day. A lot of people were incensed because I worked full-time after I got married, without being paid. He said he thought it was easier to explain. "I think we'll get along on one salary," he said. "If not, she can go to work for somebody else."

The Governor had certain things he believed in. We had a very small staff. Yet we had an efficient staff. In a period of just a few years, the Governor turned back a million dollars in untaken staff appropriations. In his thirty-four years, the amount was easily well over two million. Easily, because he turned back stationery money, too. We never used our full quota of stationery. When we wanted pads we didn't go down and buy the expensive ones. We would take obsolete stationery and have them make it into pads and buy em back for fifteen cents, which was very cheap.

It wasn't because he was stingy. He thought it was the taxpayers' money. The Governor was very conscious of that.

He *was* frugal. He always lived in a room at the Carroll Arms and shared a bathroom with a member of Congress. He saved money out of his salary. Now they say they can't afford to live down there. But he could because he didn't live like a millionaire.

His last campaign cost only $17.09. He was furious at me because someone from Vermont wrote to me and asked if I would send up some petitions. It was a Democrat. I sent them; they cost me something like $4.50 to mail. The Governor said, "Why didn't you tell em to go to Montpelier and that would have been $4.50 off the $17?" [*Laughter.*] I *mean* he was frugal.

He was an Independent in many ways. The Governor could always see the other side of the question. That's why he loved the Aiken Lectures at the University of Vermont. He wanted young people to hear both sides of the question. He used to say that things weren't black or white but gray. And he used to talk about compromises all the time. He said, "You have to compromise; otherwise you get nothing. You have to compromise because everybody feels a certain way." If I'd get mad about why someone voted a certain way, he'd say, "If we lived in his state, that's probably the way we'd vote, too."

In the Governor's day, people were more themselves. Now you watch a politician and he'll take off his coat, loosen his tie, and put his coat over his shoulder. It looks like he's really macho. They all do the same thing. And people say, "Isn't he bright!" He's probably a dodo. So many public officials now are working on their image all the time that they're not doing what they were elected to do. We never had PR or press people in our office. If the press wanted something, they went direct to the Governor.

He went everywhere in Vermont. He loved it. When he was campaigning, we never had a complete meal in one place. He would stop here and have something and there something. He never liked rallies. He always said if you went to a Republican rally, all you met were Republicans. He wanted to meet *people.* He loved going into diners and talking with people. He never had to have a Vermont office to find out what people were thinking because when he was home he wandered down the street and people talked to him. He always said it was cheaper to call him or to write a letter and get to him direct rather than go through a staff who then relayed what was said.

He reflected Vermont's ruralness and was very sympathetic to farmers. I remember his talking to one of the little girls in the office who went in to tell him that her father could not make a go as a farmer. This was years ago. The Governor said to her, "How many cows does your dad have?" And she said, "Ten." He said, "What else does he have on the farm?" And she said, "Nothing." He said, "Jenny, if each one of those cows made a profit of a thousand dollars, your dad could not live on ten thousand. He's either got to increase his herd or he's going to have to diversify a bit—maple syrup, wood, Christmas trees."

Another thing he warned about was starting in farming and

thinking you had to have all the best equipment. He said you can't afford it; you have to go in piecemeal.

He also said you can never get a group of farmers to agree among themselves, so how can you legislate for them?

The Governor was a shy person. I talked about that to another senator one time and he said that most people in public life are basically shy. The Governor would show that shyness sometimes in restaurants when people would come up to him and say, "Aren't you Senator Aiken?" You'd see just a kind of a drawing in. Then he'd say, "I used to be." Then he would start talking. He was shy, but he loved people.

I think part of it must have come from living on the farm and being a farm person—not exposed to what city children are exposed to while growing up. He always used to have to work awfully hard. He talked about having to do things for his father. Taking care of the cows and cutting wood.

But he loved people and they loved him. I remember one time when a group of consitituents wanted to come down because they were mad about something in the Senate. The Governor was on the other side from what they wanted but, he said, 'Fine, come on down and see me." When they got there, he had coffee and dough-nuts for them, which sorta disarmed them. [*Laughter.*]

I remember Ralph Nader going in to see him in favor of a con-sumer department. When he came out, the Governor had not changed his mind. The Governor told him that there were five agencies with consumer divisions and that we did not need another consumer department. But when Ralph Nader camed out, he said to me: "Take care of the Governor; we need him." It struck me so funny.

I think that's the way he affected people. Elevator boys would say to me, "You know Mrs. Aiken, you've got the most wonderful husband." I'd say, "Well the other senators are nice, too." "Oh, they're not like him; he treats us just like people." I think the Gover-nor treated Lyndon Johnson the way he treated the elevator opera-tors. I think this is what people loved about him.

The Governor was popular with presidents. FDR didn't like him for a long time because when the Governor was governor he prevented him from putting a Green Mountain highway on top of our mountains. But in his last term, he used to call the Governor down a lot. Mrs. Roosevelt was very fond of the Governor and included him in a great many things.

Of course, the Governor was very fond of Truman because he was another early bird and both of them came to the Senate very early in the morning. The Governor used to go down to the White House a lot when Truman was there.

I think probably Lyndon Johnson was one of his favorites because Lyndon Johnson always gave him everything he wanted. I think it went back to LBJ's first heart attack when he was in the Senate. The Governor wrote to him faithfully every week. Lyndon Johnson always remembered those things—what you did to him, whether it was good or bad. And he liked the Governor. Of course, Lyndon Johnson got very mad at him when he made the statement that he thought we should declare that we'd won the war and withdraw slowly. For months after that, the Governor was not invited to the White House.

I remember being at Enosburg after the Governor's retirement. They had a marathon at the Dairy Festival and a young boy eighteen years old won it. The master of ceremonies asked the boy if he'd like to speak to the crowd. There were a lot of people there, but the boy said, No, what he'd really like to do—he'd always wanted to shake Senator Aiken's hand. The Governor had no idea what a compliment that was to him. That an eighteen-year-old would want to shake his hand. I said, "An eighteen-year-old usually doesn't give a damn about a public official."

The Governor had that influence on young people. In his book, *Speaking from Vermont*, there's a passage where he says, "If you give young people responsibility, they will rise to it."

When he died, I got wonderful letters from around the country. One of the nicest cards was signed by everybody in the Senate custodian's office. Which tells you something. He was remembered by people because people weren't afraid of him as they are of a lot of public officials.

Mary Arthur

GRANGER

Burlington, Vermont
Born: 1905

➤➤➤➤➤➤➤➤➤➤➤➤➤➤➤➤ ✳ ◄◄◄◄◄◄◄◄◄◄◄◄◄◄◄◄

THE GRANGE IS ONE OF THE MOST widespread institutions in Vermont. After the Civil War, a New Englander named Oliver Hudson Kelly proposed creation of a nationwide fraternity of rural people that would both aid reconstruction and educate the American farmer. Because Kelly was an active Mason, this new fraternal order developed a complex system of degrees and offices: master, overseer, lecturer, steward, assistant steward, lady assistant steward, deputy, chaplain, and gatekeeper. The first Vermont Grange, Green Mountain No. 1, was started in the old Union schoolhouse in St. Johnsbury on December 4, 1866. The order quickly spread across the state.

Grange officers with Harold Arthur (left) and Mary Arthur (right)

14

Amidst all the formal titles, the essence of Grange work consists of covered-dish suppers, slide shows, rural education, visits to shut-ins, field trips, and other good works. Mary Arthur has been a member since 1930 and has held many local, state, and national offices. It is fitting that, in keeping with the social nature of the Grange, she met her husband, former governor Harold J. Arthur, through local meetings in Burlington.

While governor in 1950, Harold Arthur was also state master of the Vermont Grange. "He knew his *Robert's Rules of Order* and was good at being the presiding officer of anything"—from the Elks Club to the American Legion to the state government. Reportedly he was most noted for his whistling ability, having whistled even for sessions of the state legislature.

The Grange is as Vermont as cows and maples. As Mary Arthur says, "It's a good organization; they believe in not starting a meeting unless the Bible is on the altar and the flag is in evidence."

I was not a farmer but I always felt very close to them. When I was working as secretary to a Burlington lawyer, the people who came in were often farmers.

The overseer of our Grange at that time lived on a farm and he was a deputy sheriff. And he said, "We're going to get you into the Grange." So I joined. I wasn't married then. At that time my future husband was a member of the Grange in Brandon, Vermont. I was in Burlington. When he transferred here, I met him.

When I joined the Grange, it had a nice class of people— teachers, a town clerk, farmers. Educated people. Anyone who was interested in agriculture. I was quickly put in charge of the Third Degree.

My husband was a very social person and very well liked. I met him at a Grange meeting. I had just won a Dodge sedan by getting the most subscriptions to a country newspaper. It was my first car and it was very nice. So I took it to the Grange. After the meeting, he said, "Where are you going?"

I said, "Going home." He didn't have a car then, so he really hinted that he wanted a ride home. I gave him a ride. After that we were friends. [*Laughter*].

In 1938 Harold was master of our Pomona Grange and I was lecturer. At that time we were both single and I did the best I could as lecturer to make an impression on him.

I was admitted to the bar before he was because he didn't start studying law until later. I had been studying from the state senator I worked for; Harold registered as a law student with U.S. ambassador Warren R. Austin.

He had two sisters. His mother was good on making their clothes and taking them around to put on plays. He'd whistle and one girl would sing and the other one would act. It was a family that went around the neighborhood and entertained people. He whistled just like a bird. A beautiful whistle. The legislature used to call him in to whistle and he whistled for various organizations. He had the name of being a very good whistler.

The Grange has been very important to me. I enjoyed it as much as my husband did. The state and the national organization treated us very, very well. I'd stick by the Grange and Grange people. They're the salt of the earth. You can depend on them. They're honest, helpful, and sincere. Even now when I go around, why you'd think that the queen was coming.

Elizabeth Brouha

ARTS ACTIVIST

Sutton, Vermont
Born: 1916

➤➤➤➤➤➤➤➤➤➤➤➤➤➤➤➤ ✪ ◄◄◄◄◄◄◄◄◄◄◄◄◄◄◄◄◄

VERMONT MAY BE MOST KNOWN elsewhere for its maples, scenery, cows, and skiing, but its children are its most valuable asset. All too often the educational needs of those children have been neglected. For instance, during the energy crisis of the early 1970s, budgetary pressures became so acute in certain Northeast Kingdom elementary schools that curricula shrank to a bare bones "readin, writin, and rithmatic." Teachers of "frills" like physical education, art, and music were given their walking papers. The victims of lost battles for educational excellence usually feel no physical pain; they do not walk with a limp. But they *are* victims nonetheless, because they are unable to achieve up to their full potential in life.

One remarkable woman, totally outside the school system, unexpectedly led a counterattack from her farm on Hardscrabble Hill near Sutton. Elizabeth Brouha has lived in Vermont since 1941; her idea that the arts are a birthright of every Northeast Kingdom child is one of those happy imports that may be as important to the state now as the horse Justin Morgan was two hundred years ago.

Elizabeth Brouha grew up in an American family in Brussels, Belgium, where she attended the experimental school of a Swiss psychiatrist named Ovide Decroly. His rigorous instructional methods, developed first on children with learning disabilities, emphasized observation and association. Children learned Latin locutions as early as first grade; school days were much longer than is common now. Art was an intrinsic part of the Ecole Decroly and students were required to illustrate everything they learned. The whole program and Ovide Decroly himself must have been very unusual. Elizabeth Brouha remembers fondly her mentor's long salt and pepper beard and his enthusiasm for teaching.

At the age of six, she also enrolled in French diction classes at the home of an inestimable lady named Mademoiselle Duval, from whom Elizabeth's mother insisted she learn a proper non-Belgian French accent, in the Academie Française style. This course consisted of the memorization and recitation of "immense amounts of French poetry." I suppose there is only so much time that can be spent perfecting pronunciation, even in a French country; the diction course soon evolved into an art course. Before long professional artists were teaching Elizabeth and her chums twice a week at a Brussels museum. "We learned that the arts were extremely important," she says. "I have benefited tremendously from the general education I had. I think it's every man's birthright to have arts in his life."

In 1970 Elizabeth Brouha saw an opportunity to rescue stately old Burklyn Hall north of St. Johnsbury from neglect and decay and to turn it into a cultural center of the type she had known in Europe. And so began the Friends of Burklyn (the word *Burklyn* combines local town names Burke and Lyndon). Concerts, lectures, and workshops of every kind soon enlivened the old mansion. School kids were bused across the Northeast Kingdom's hills to that scenic old home high between two branches of the Passumpsic River.

Despite all the enthusiasm and the fundraisers and the crafts fairs, the cultural center failed to win state support. But when that cause fizzled, the Friends of Burklyn merely moved their booming art education activities into the elementary schools. There Elizabeth and her friends developed a three-year cycle of Artists-in-Residence programs. They offered creative writing one year and then visual arts and then music and drama. Through repetitions of this cycle, every child had the opportunity to go through the program twice during his first six years of school.

Alan Davis, Artists-in-Residence coordinator of the Vermont Council on the Arts, calls Elizabeth Brouha "a wonderful person who has laid the groundwork for a wider view of the world." He says that "Vermont is characterized by limited resources for the arts in the schools, especially in the Northeast Kingdom. She has turned around a poor situation and enriched the lives of kids. She has brought in a wide range of artists and projects in all the important disciplines. For kids in small rural schools, these have been the only artistic opportunities. Her hard work on fundraising and scheduling has made flowers bloom in our cultural desert (or tundra). Instead of being victims of television, the possibilities of the world have been opened to those kids. She has not only led them but also school administrators and the public and has built a foundation for the arts in the community."

Elizabeth Brouha says that the whole thing evolved from her own education at the Ecôle Decroly and in the art course of Mademoiselle Duval.

"It was so important to me," she says, "to be taught by professional artists and not just ordinary school teachers. My own grown children have a hard time understanding why I knock myself out now doing all this work. But I can't keep myself from doing it.

"I feel that those kids are deprived and that they've *got* to have art in their lives."

We started off young by illustrating everything we learned. Art was part of our school's everyday life, but it was reinforced for me because I also went to an art course which, when it outgrew Mademoiselle Duval's house, was held in the history and archaeology museum in Bruxelles. We art students who went there every Tuesday and Thursday afternoon had the run of the museum—its Egyptian, Greco-Roman, oriental, and prehistoric art sections. It was a rich experience. For instance, we had prehistoric art, drawing animals the way prehistoric people did on their cave walls at Lascaux and other places. We worked up through the ages with art from all over the world. We created things in the manner of the Japanese or the Chinese or the Greeks or the Egyptians. Our own ideas were expressed in their ways and using their art restrictions.

I enjoyed it tremendously. As a consequence I learned a lot about visual arts. When I was a high schooler at the museum—with a nice big studio with north light—Mademoiselle Duval brought in well-known artists to teach us. We did oils with Cromelynck and we did etchings with his cousin and we went through the whole gamut of printmaking. All of these important artists would come in and teach us, sort of like the Artists-in-Residence program we have now at our schools.

Back in 1975, when the local tax base shrank, they threw out all the art teachers and music teachers. We didn't have any for years. With the tax base diminishing, the schools decided it would be better to spend their money on what they called the "basics" to the exclusion of "frills" like the arts. My feeling was that those things were not frills at all and that they were extremely important. Many kids here had never participated in a lively way in anything intellectual in school. They were dummies, perhaps because they were too scared to open their mouths.

But when our poets come in for residencies, those children open up. Not only to language and to playing with words but also to a

Elizabeth Brouha (center)

multitude of other things. And because they suddenly wake up, they succeed much better in everything.

Most people will deny that the arts are the most basic of all basics. But after all, man started out with art long before he learned to write or to count.

I'm trying to get these youngsters to feel the joy of doing something with their own hands and of imagining things. To liberate their imaginations, which are now captivated by all this television and buncombe. Our kids lack the imagination that is the right of every human. They don't have the joy of having an object in their hands that they have made. I think it's a very important part of life to be able to say "I made this."

Kids respond extremely well to the Artists-in-Residence experience.

Jim Doyle is the president of Friends of Burklyn; he is also a teacher of creative writing here at Lyndon State College. He went to a lot of very good schools and has all kinds of degrees. He and his wife lived in the vicinity of New York City. He has two sons, including Joshua, who is in high school now. Joshua was having awful difficulties in the city schools. His parents had him tested and the educational counselors said he was hopeless, that he would never learn a damn thing. And Josh was very, very unhappy because he couldn't read and he was in a terrible state. He was lost.

Jim and his wife decided it would help to leave greater New York and go as far away as possible to the boonies; they came to the Northeast Kingdom. They now live in the tiny town of Sutton where I live.

Joshua was sent to the local school, a small one with about one hundred twenty-five students in kindergarten through grade eight. Joshua was very much more comfortable there because he had kind teachers. It's a nice school. The kids like each other and the teachers like the kids and each other. I'm invariably very well received there. All the kids in town know me and call me Elizabeth. It's a very nice feeling.

And so Joshua was getting on fairly well, but not all that well, when Friends of Burklyn brought in a poet to be with the children for a whole week, visiting each grade and doing poetry with them. Because the poet was also a printer, the outcome of the residency was a book of poetry from not only that school but also the Burke, Sheffield, and Wheelock schools. Our plan in that year of creative writing was to teach the kids not only poetry and the fun of using words but also how paper is made, how books are put together and bound, and what the various kinds of alphabets are throughout the world. It was a lot of fun and very fruitful.

We put together a little book. There were enough that we could give one to each of the school kids. When the books were distributed toward the end of the school year, Joshua was given his book. He looked through it hastily and he found his name and his poem.

His reaction was to shoot out of his chair and to run down the street shouting, "My poem's in the book. My poem's in the book."

His parents live right in town. When he dashed indoors, they were both at home. He was brandishing his book and calling out for all the town to hear, "My poem is in the book. My poem is in the book."

And they fell on each other and hugged each other. And everybody started crying and it was great.

Josh's father, a teacher of creative writing, was so tickled with the whole thing that he wrote a letter to Ellen Levell at the Vermont Council on the Arts about the whole experience. Ellen was going down to Washington, D. C. to plead that more money be given to the National Endowment for the Arts so that the state councils could have more money for programs like this. She went before a committee and read them Joshua's poem and his father's letter. It was the greatest thing on the program. It carried the day and the Endowment did get more money.

And that's the story of Joshua's howling success.

Mervil Bruleigh

DEPUTY SHERIFF

East Corinth, Vermont
Born: 1907

>>>>>>>>>>>>>>>>>>>>> ⊛ <<<<<<<<<<<<<<<<<<<<<

MERVIL BRULEIGH IS DEPUTY SHERIFF of Orange County. He smokes a corn-cob pipe—"hard to find good ones now," he says; operates radar traps; catches nude swimmers; and generally looks like Jackie Gleason should be playing his part. His advice to young people is to get off drugs and to join the Masons. His stories hark back to a Victorian era when the established order must have seemed preordained.

Nostalgia is a central part of our pleasure in thinking about Vermont. But I hope that this book, in addition to being country store full of memories, will also be a nettle ready to spur discussions about the relative value of past and present. Mervil Bruleigh, for instance, believes in the remembered different-ness of the Champlain Islanders of his youth. What about those differences and the differences between Vermonters and other Americans yesterday and today?

Deputy sheriff Bruleigh's heroes were wealthy lairds, an unexpected, to me, source of inspiration in egalitarian Vermont. Frederick Wells, for one, owned Stave Island and employed four men—captain, deckhand, cook, and engineer— just to run his boat. Another hero was a self-made squire named Mose Brown whose bobbin-making inventions once sustained the village of East Corinth, where Officer Bruleigh has lived for many years. Mervil liked that factory owner's "honesty and generosity to the poor."

Honesty is the central Bruleigh theme. Once Mervil made one of his sons return an ear of corn the boy had taken from a neighbor's fields. The neighbor protested that it was not necessary to shame the boy that way over such a small thing, but Mervil was adamant.

When the deputy sheriff was himself a boy, the Champlain Islands in Grand Isle County were famous for "some of the best farming in North America." Apples, cherries, peas, beans: "You could raise anything down there." South Hero was like "one big family" with only two or three hundred people, all of them extremely honest, according to Mervil.

Deputy sheriff Bruleigh will soon retire at the age of seventy nine. I hope it is a peaceful retirement; he has seen too much dishonesty. But would it have been better if he had stayed in the islands? Are there any refuges left for the truly honest person? "We don't find too many young fellas growing up today that . . . I'd hate to trust any one of em." Officer Bruleigh says, "There's a few that you can, but most of em are into marijuana or into cocaine or something else. That's what worries me. My grandchildren are growing up and they're right down in the school where it is. Our hands are tied. I don't think we're ever going to lick this dope business until we get a law that will allow us to do a search."

Diogenes need not have searched the world for an honest man had he met Officer Bruleigh.

Once his hero Mr. Wells told some strolling ladies they should watch for cowslips on the path. Honest young Mervil piped up, "That's not cowslips; that's cow shit."

"Mr. Wells had a great laugh out of that," says Mervil. "He knew what I'd say."

Most of the people who came from the islands were considered to be different. They were more honest. Where I was brought up down in the islands, in South Hero and Grand Isle County, there was like one big family.

In 1909 my folks moved from Burlington, Vermont to a seventy-five-acre island out in Lake Champlain three miles from any land. I was two years old when they went there and they were there for four and a half years. I remember about everything that went on. My mother kept a diary that tells everything that happened every day of the week. How cold it was. How hard the south wind blew. And how foggy.

Stave Island was owned by Frederick Wells. He was the Wells of Wells and Richardson Diamond Dyes. My dad, I guess, was maybe the third caretaker he had there. Mr. Wells married when he was thirty-eight years old and he was probably forty four when we knew him.

They built a seventy-five-foot tower on that island on the highest spot. And they built a new barn. I was there this summer and the steps that my dad built in 1910 are still there going up to the tower. And the barn is just as perfect as the day it was built in 1910.

Mervil Bruleigh

On that island there were three cows, a horse, and around forty-five to fifty deer. There was a fourteen-foot fence around the island to keep the deer in. I was really brought up with the deer. My dad had one that he bottle fed and grew it up as a pet.

In the fall of 1912 Mr. Wells shot fourteen buck deer. The big boat on Lake Champlain then was the *Ticonderoga.* It's in the Shelburne Museum now. They loaded them fourteen deer on it and they went to Burlington to the meat market.

Mrs. Wells had a pet deer she used to feed sugar. Three years or so after we moved off, the deer went berserk and attacked a man. The fella got out of it OK. But next spring they let that deer out of his enclosure and he attacked that man again and gored the horse and two of the cows. Mr. Wells shot every one of them buck and the next winter all them deer were let go on the ice.

Mr. Wells was a wonderful man. He looked after my folks pretty good there. In the fall we would have a big barrel of sugar. A big barrel of flour. Maybe a hundred pounds of lard. And all kinds of potatoes on hand.

The only thing was that if one of us broke an arm . . . I have a scar here where a dog bit me one summer. I crawled through a fence and my dog tried to follow and got stuck. I went back three times to lift him out of that fence and he bit me every damn time. I'll never forget that. They took me to Providence Island, almost three miles away. There was a Colonel Nelson Jackson who owned that and he was a doctor. I can remember him heating a wire up and going down where the dog bit and burning that out.

Today I pick these damn dogs up that somebody dumps off. No collar on em and you don't know if they've had a rabies shot or not. I've been bit three or four times but I've been lucky.

People coming from the islands were different. Because if somebody did something wrong down there, it wasn't like it is up around here where they can break into a house and get caught and think nothing about it.

But down there if somebody did something like that, if he stole even a small thing, nobody would have anything to do with him. They'd barely speak to him.

That person was ostracized.

Jay Craven

IMPRESARIO

St. Johnsbury, Vermont
Born: 1950

➤➤➤➤➤➤➤➤➤➤➤➤➤➤➤➤ ⊛ ◄◄◄◄◄◄◄◄◄◄◄◄◄◄◄◄◄

VERMONT, DESPITE THE STEREOTYPES, IS never static. Nor is it ever truly isolated from the bigger world around it. The state evolved out of the land
grant conflict between New Hampshire and New York and between the
rebellious thirteen colonies and Britain's imperial policies. Just before the
Civil War, distant happenings were noisily present as church bells tolled
the death of John Brown. Almost every town has its veterans memorial.
National events and state history are always closely intertwined. And that
leads me to the subject of the post–World War II baby boomers and the
young impresario of St. Johnsbury, Vermont.

Esquire magazine's 1984 issue about outstanding leaders aged forty and
younger included a long Ann Beattie article about Jay Craven, founder of
the Northeast Kingdom's nonprofit Catamount Film & Arts. Jay was
active in "the movement," as sixties people used to say, and settled in Vermont to continue the old struggles in new ways, primarily by making serious performing art available to Northeast Kingdom audiences. During my
visit, he and his collaborators were transforming an old post office into a
performance hall for Catamount Arts.

Jay Craven's progress as arts pilgrim took him from boyhood in a broken
Pennsylvania family to war-torn Vietnam as a nineteen-year-old student
leader, to organizing John Lennon's aborted antiwar tour and participation
in the Manhattan arts world. This baby boom Everyman is an articulate,
determined promoter of the arts in a place where sophisticates might
expect only lowbrow entertainment. I attended a performance by an
innovative yet accessible French puppet company and came away wishing
I could have seen the whole season's line-up of music and drama.

As befits someone who derived personal and generational identity from
the Vietnam, Watergate, and assassination era of the sixties and early

seventies, Jay Craven says that "those experiences that were most influential for me were those that demystified or revealed something about my assumptions. Assumptions based on my ambition or my sense of direction at a particular moment. To have that thrown off base. To have to look at something newly. To redirect energy."

Because "a healthy, vital society is one that can reexamine its assumptions and change," Jay Craven's productions seek to "offer a shared moment between artist and audience" within a kind of confrontation about the issues of perception, of feeling, and of our times. I am fascinated that through this one fellow's life, and the multiple inspirations that go into it, the boundaries are being fudged between art and politics in Vermont. Jay Craven says, "We cannot be hippies trying to live on sixties energies and ideas—you take what is good and try to integrate it into your next step."

Vermont as a nonmaterialistic state too poor to afford Sun Belt hedonism has been and can be a significant haven for creativity. Consider the Marlboro Festival in southern Vermont, the Bread and Puppet Theater in the northeast, and the exciting work being done by artists and writers everywhere from the Molly Stark Trail to the Quebec border.

I hope that Vermonters with their long tradition of independent-mindedness will welcome and debate Jay Craven's productions with all the enthusiasm of tent-goers at a nineteenth-century Chautauqua. "What we are trying to do is establish an authentic community-based arts organization that stimulates free exchange of ideas and creative expression," he says. "And try to get stuff to the schools and to populations that aren't normally exposed to the arts."

Bravo! Bravo!

I think that sometimes kids in broken families tend to become more philosophical about where they stand in relation to the world. I was inspired by a father I hardly knew and a grandfather and grandmother I lived with in eastern Pennsylvania after the split-up of my parents. When I was six, my parents divorced; I never saw my father again. When I was seventeen, I learned that he had committed suicide. I think growing up without my natural father tended to cause me as a young boy to fantasize a lot about what I would be and how I might hold that up relative to what my unknown father would think. He became a sort of phantom to measure my progress against. I had no contact with the real person but nonetheless I wanted to prove something.

My grandfather was a charismatic and forthright and outgoing personality who also influenced me. He died when I was nine. I continue to think a lot about him.

The election of Kennedy in 1960 had an inspirational influence on me. It swept up the whole country. Even though I was only ten years old, world tensions being what they were, there was a sense of momentum. Then three years later came the assassination of Kennedy; at that point I was thirteen years old. There was the whole feeling of being caught up with events.

That all caused me to become interested in politics. When you have great and successful artists, more young people decide to become artists. When you have politicians who are ascendent and political activism growing, more people become interested in politics.

As an activist, I was involved with and influenced by Chicago Seven activists Rennie Davis and Dave Dellinger. Davis was an extremely charasmatic speaker and organizer, who later led me on a filmmaking expedition expedition to Vietnam via India, where he defected to the entourage of the fifteen-year-old Guru Maharaj Ji. Dellinger remains a close friend and a committed activist, espousing a lifetime commitment to social change through non-violence.

All of the influences I've talked about so far were a little bit fleeting and elusive. And each of them was flawed. My father whom I didn't know inspired me in an abstract way. What I do know of him is that when he died he was alcoholic and unmotivated. My grandfather was fairly successful but certainly a flawed personality. Likewise Kennedy. As I became older, I came to understand some of Kennedy's duplicity and compromising and bad faith. Likewise my activist involvements were frequently frustrating for a variety of reasons, though I continue to believe in progressive social change.

I think that my generation grew up through those times being inspired, then disillusioned in the next breath. And that's what stimulated some of the activism in the sixties. I think it was the loss of leaders or mentors to believe in, both from disillusionment and from assassination, which led us to believe more in ourselves and in group involvement.

Coming out of high school inspired by Martin Luther King, Jr. and by Bobby Kennedy, I actively looked at them as people to admire. But each of them fell away. As I became older and became more aware, things again became demystified.

People began to influence me artistically in high school. Seeing an art film for the first time—Antonioni's *Blow-Up*, at a drive-in movie when I was sixteen years old—was a tremendous inspiration to me. I was inspired, too, by T. S. Eliot's poetry and by seeing Ferlinghetti read live. My perception of art became to help people see with new eyes. To look at things in a completely different light.

Going to college at Boston University I found that I was inspired by my peers. People who were doing interesting things artistically and politically. I became part of a group and very interested in what was going on. I made my first film while I was a freshman in college. I became active in student government. As student body president, I got involved in representing the United States National Student Association and went to Vietnam when I was nineteen years old, which was a big opening up for me. That experience in some ways frightened me because it seemed so large an undertaking. Also, knowing of our plan to meet with student leaders from both North Vietnam and South Vietnam and what that might do for my personal ambition in politics. At the same time, it was a demystifying experience.

You do need to be open to change. I think that's where the two influences, the artistic and the political, overlap.

I've gone through changes in my life; the value of commitment is something I've come to know more about. Living here you see families enduring the changes in the seasons and in the economy. People here require certain enduring, rock-ribbed principles. I've come to value more those things that last and that have an ongoing legacy. That's partly the reason why in my work at Catamount I've tried to sink its roots deeply into the community and tried to develop the work in a way that is authentic to the community.

At the same time I'm probably a weirdo here in other regards. Probably a lot of people would view me that way. But we are able to accomplish things that people respect and respond to. I'm able to play the role of the gadfly and present events and make films that are intended to provoke fresh response.

We don't want Catamount to be predictable. As we become stronger, we want to give a voice to an increasing number of artists and their art forms, especially locally, to enable young people to develop artistic expression. Also to bring artists in from outside who are unlike anything people have ever seen here before.

Last night we had a performance of the Negro Ensemble Company doing *A Soldier's Play*. A very provocative play dealing with issues of being black in the segregated military in World War II. We had a full-house Northeast Kingdom audience of people who don't see black people very often. But there was a real edge to the moment. That's what presenting the arts is. What you are offering is a shared moment *between* artist and audience. And *among* the audience, particularly in a community where the audience knows each other pretty well. Through that artistic performance, we had a successful moment, a kind of confrontation on the issues.

There are many people like myself who have a vision of the way they would like to see society and are actively trying to make society that way through concrete steps. In all fields — health, education, politics, the arts . . . I think people who have done that have been influenced by a multiplicity of mentors and ideas. Certainly that's the case with me. But it's just as important to be constantly demystifying those forces, not take them or yourself too seriously. Instead of modeling ourselves on somebody, we should be transforming and adapting to meet the challenges of today.

My newest inspiration is my two-and-a-half-year-old boy. When I look at his perceptions and his needs, my greatest challenge is to meet those needs and to be honest with him. That's the way he is with me.

Vermont has a traditional conservatism that is the old style of conservatism, which basically says that for things to change they should change only for good reason.

But once the good reason is presented, things do change.

There is an openness in Vermont by people to respect all points of view. That's a very strongly held belief here.

Agnes Deering

POSTMISTRESS AND POET LAUREATE

Guildhall, Vermont
Born: 1919

>>>>>>>>>>>>>>>>> ⊗ <<<<<<<<<<<<<<<<<<

THE LOWLY DANDELION

The fields are alive with dandelions
  Their blossoms a beautiful golden hue,
Called a weed by all the farmers
  Making them fret and stew.

I wonder if ever they realize
  The wonderful foods they bring?
Yes, the lowly unsung dandelion
  That grows so well in early spring.

The leaves are fine in a tossed salad
  Or cooked with ham as an early green,
Tiny blossom buds covered with cheese sauce
  Really taste like a delectable dream.

The blossoms can be used for many things
  Like cough syrup, jellies and wine,
Also dipped in egg batter and floured
  Fried in butter a very short time.

So please, Mr. Farmer, don't deny us
  This gift from Heaven on high,
As on the soft winds of springtime
  The seeds of the dandelion fly.

AGNES DEERING, THE POET LAUREATE of Guildhall, Vermont, has been writing poems ever since she was "knee-high to a grasshopper." Officially she is the postmistress of her remote Northeast Kingdom town on the Connecticut River. True to the best Vermont tradition, her post office was originally in Mrs. Stevens's country store, but for the last year Agnes Deering has had a small, tidy federal building all to herself. "This is all insulated and everything," she says proudly. "Electric heat. Running water. Bathroom."

Because Depression-era Guildhall was a railroad town, many hobos passed through on their endless boxcar travels in search of work. Word spread up and down the tracks that Agnes's grandmother was always ready to give a hungry man something to eat. Agnes, who lived upstairs, would always answer her grandmother's tap on the pipes and be present for those impromptu dinners of potatoes and wild greens, fried dandelions, cowslips, and more.

She also remembers when her grandmother's family would come down to visit from Quebec. "Some couldn't talk English. Only French. So the others would have to explain what they were talking about. It was a lot of fun."

Agnes's mother worked in a mill for nine dollars a week. Money was so short that the little girl went to school in secondhand clothes, to the derision of some of her classmates. The future poet laureate organized her fellow victims to get A's in order to show up the hecklers.

Like her grandmother, Agnes Deering is a giver. She was a 4-H leader for eighteen years and town clerk and treasurer for nine years. She served eighteen years on the school board. Despite her hard life, she is much more than a survivor. She, like her grandmother, brightens the lives of the people around her. "I like to talk to people and be friendly with people," she says cheerily. "I was taught to do that."

She is also ready to impart dandelion wisdom to all comers. Dandelion wine. Dandelion blossom jelly. Fried dandelion blossoms. To make her child-pleasing dandelion cough syrup, she advises boiling fifteen dandelion blossoms for each cup of water. Cool, strain, and add one-half cup of sugar for each cup of liquid. Then boil again until it is syrupy.

That syrup is probably like the poems she produces on demand for birthdays, weddings, and anniversaries: homemade, sweet, and personal.

Recently, a man named McLean summed up the magic of Agnes Deerings's post office to me as he was leaving with his mail: "This is the place to meet anybody, that's for sure. And you can usually find out what's going on in the village once you come over here and spend a few minutes. It's a joy to come here every day, even if you don't pick up mail."

Agnes Deering

My mother had to work and bring up two kids on nine dollars a week. So we spent a lot of time with Grammy and she taught me most everything I know.

Grammy got me into everything edible, anything we could eat. Apples or plants—we'd always go out and get em. And we'd dig dandelions. Of course, we had feeds, and dandelions last quite awhile. We'd run over to the old company store and get a piece of salt pork to cook with em.

We'd eat anything else we could find that was edible. We used to pick cowslip greens. They have a beautiful yellow flower and grow in the swamps.

Grammy was always good to everybody. She used to fix these things for the hobos and bums who came on the freight trains. They'd come to her house and ask her for something to eat. Once they found out where they could get it, they all showed up. We would help Grammy to fix something for em to eat.

If she was home alone when my grandfather was away working, she'd rap on the pipe—we lived upstairs—and one of us would go down and stay with her so she wouldn't be alone with the hobos.

She always took care of them. I remember grandfather coming home and he'd look in the cupboard and he'd say, "Oh yes, I know they've been here again," because the cupboards would be pretty near bare. [*Laughter.*]

There was a fair down here at Lancaster every year. We couldn't afford to go, so we'd pick raspberries and blackberries and sell em to earn money for the fair. Grammy would always tell us where the best place was to get em.

Any time anyone was sick they'd always call on Grammy. She'd tell em what to do or she would take care of em herself. I remember one of my cousins had pneumonia; the doctor said there wasn't a thing they could do for her. A little baby. And Grammy said, "You bring her here." So they brought her up to Grammy's house and she made a mustard plaster to put on that little baby. Mustard plaster is made of ground mustard. It can get powerful hot. You've got to be awful careful or you'll burn the skin right off. But it works.

That mustard plaster had to be changed every three hours. Well, she was going to stay up day and night taking care of that baby, but we told her that we'd do it at night. Every three hours my aunt and I would get up and change that mustard plaster. Now that little baby has grandchildren of her own. But that doctor had said there wasn't anything anybody could do for her.

Grammy used to give us hot ginger tea with warm milk in it for colds. We called it hot because she put so much ginger in it that the ginger would burn all the way down. Oh, it was fun!

I remember one time when a family's car broke down in the middle of winter. They had two little kids and it was desperately cold. They asked if the wife and little kids could stay at Grammy's while the husband went to get the car fixed. So I went downstairs and we fed em and held the little babies. Then when they got ready to go, Grammy took her sweater off—she only had one sweater—and insisted on that woman bundling up her little baby. The woman said, "I can't take your sweater."

And Grammy said, "Look, you've got to keep that little one warm."

She always did that. If she could give anything to anybody, she always did. She was something extra special.

She always had a great big thick Bible beside her bed. It had the most beautiful pictures. Even before I learned how to read, I would go in and look at those pictures. I'd ask her what they meant and she would always explain em out to me. After I got so I could read and write, I would read that Bible to her.

She could read printing, but she couldn't write. Her sister and her other folks lived up in Canada and she was always having me write letters to them.

Grammy's people were from Canada. On my father's side, some of his came over from England on the Maytag, I mean Mayflower.

My great-grandmother on my father's side was a full-blooded Indian who used to live up here on Guildhall Hill. Then I had some that was mixed up with the Irish.

My grandmother's name was Ellen Hampton. Her first husband was killed when lightning hit him when he was loading some hay on a wagon. So Grammy, everytime there was a thunder shower, she'd get her rocking chair and set in that and us kids had to gather around her. We couldn't go get a drink of water or anything else. We had to stay right there 'cause she was awful afraid of lightning.

Grammy died quite a few years ago when tuberculosis was going around town. And, boy, that was an awful letdown.

This was a railroad town. The station was right down behind my house.

The hobos were trying to find jobs. They would go from one town to another; they would stop where they could get something to eat. I remember there was a man who owned the big hotel in Groveton and this old fella came along and asked him for a dime. That hotel owner hauled off and knocked that poor fellow flat right up against a cement wall. Boy, was I ever mad! I ran all the way down the street and called a cop. All he did was put that poor old man in jail. He never said a thing to the hotel owner. Oh, I thought that was terrible!

There are a lot of people who still condemn this one or that one and I don't think it's fair. We had some people here once who were very poor and who also had to wear secondhand clothes and who couldn't dress up for Sunday school. So the Sunday school teacher finally said, "I don't think I'll let them come to Sunday school anymore."

I said, "Why not?"

"Well, because they don't look like the other kids."

I said, "Don't let that make any difference. If they want to learn about God and Christ, let em come to Sunday school. It doesn't matter what they've got on."

Grammy always told us never to condemn anybody until you walk in their shoes. She said, "You never know why they are like that until you live their life and find out." She was a grand old lady, I'm telling you!

People think the Northeast Kingdom is very backward; *I* think that smells to high heaven. We have some very good people around here. When I was on the 4-H one time, we were going to Washington, D.C. and some Vermonter asked where I was from.

"Guildhall," I said.

"Where's that?"

I said, "It's the forgotten end of the Kingdom." I thought it was terrible they didn't know little old Guildhall.

The people who live around here—Guildhall, Maidstone, Lunenburg, Gilman—are a nice group of friendly people. They are always willing to help somebody. And they don't hold out their hand and say, "Gimme, gimme, gimme." They work for a living. That's why I take off my hat to them.

I have a ball with the little kids when they come in the post office. They always want to see Aggie. I give em a little sticker to put on their hands or something like that. I often have people calling to find out where somebody lives and I help them. Sometimes people say, "My gosh. Usually I go in a post office to buy a stamp and they throw it at me and turn their backs. You never do that. You talk to us."

And I say, "Why not? You're paying my salary."

Orien Dunn

PUMP LOG BORER AND BLACKSMITH

Granby, Vermont
Born: 1901

>->->->->->->->->->->->->->- ⊛ -<-<-<-<-<-<-<-<-<-<-<-<-<-<-<

BEFORE PLASTIC PIPE WAS widely available, wood was the cheapest Vermont material for use in making water pipes. A pump log is the hollowed-out timber through which water flowed from outdoor springs and pumps indoors. When pump-log borer Orien Dunn explains the process of making one, it all sounds deceptively simple. As he says, "You don't have to go far in this country before you can find logs enough." After cutting the right-size trees, he hollows them out with a long-handled auger, sharpens one log end like a pencil, and indents the other to fit its neighbor. Presto! A pump log.

Of course, the ordinary person could easily go wrong. A common mistake occurs when the borer does not remove the wood shavings that quickly accumulate inside the opening. When the auger freezes in the clogged hole there is only one solution: shamefacedly chopping the log apart to free the tool.

Orien Dunn hails from the Northeast Kingdom's remote village of Granby. His shop there is a local landmark in which every square inch of wall space is covered with license plates. You couldn't miss Orien Dunn himself because his chest-length white beard causes him to resemble an Old Testament prophet.

The photograph shows Orien Dunn demonstrating pump-log boring at the Fairbanks Museum in St. Johnsbury. He is eager to pass the skill on the same way he learned it from his blacksmith, jack-of-all-trades father. Orien told me that if I got "tied up too tight," I should come to see him for more advice. "I'll help anybody who wants to make history," he said.

Orien Dunn

We put em in the ground for the water to run through to the house from a spring. We take a log eight foot long and at least eight inches at the butt end and bore a hole straight through. Fir balsam. Cedar makes good logs but it's damn hard to find.

When I was seventeen, eighteen years old I was boring logs with my dad and he got cramped up in some way and I took over. And I went about twelve, fourteen miles to the next job and got over there by gee whiz and I went and cut the trees in the woods. I took my horse and hauled them all out of the woods into a bunch. Then I cut the big end off all of em so they were perfectly flat.

If we have a log cut to the dimensions that we want, and if it's laid up on horses as we call em and dogged down so that log can't move, then we bore right through there eight feet. Then we got a riggin that I stick in that hole and I turn it around three or four times and that makes a tunnel in each end. Over on the other end, you make it down so it'll fit that tunnel. That's the way you put your logs together.

Dad would go out into the neighborhood and help lay water pipe with lead pipe. He'd put them right in the ground and keep adding on until they got to the house. But he didn't like them. If you've ever noticed, lead pipe has got a scale on it inside and out. In my part of the country, we were trying to get all fir logs in for water and get rid of that damn slime inside.

My dad was a blacksmith for horses and for any ironwork that needed to be repaired. It didn't make no odds whether it was for horseshoes or what it was. Latches and hinges up to the size for a barn door.

I don't know that he ever made an auger by hand. I know that he used to go to Glover, Vermont. There was a man up there that made em. That was his business. He didn't make anything else. Dad would go up there and buy the bits and bring em home and weld em onto iron of his own to make his auger to bore with.

The auger is an inch-and-a-quarter bit. It goes around like that once. Then it straightens out about two feet. Then there's a solid iron welded into that that goes back to the handle that you turn.

My father was born and brought up right there in the town of Granby. My mother was born there, too, and went to the same one-room school. They got married when they got out of school.

I took my dad for my model as far as anything went that I could do. As long as I was doing any work, I tried to get as close to the same as he was as I could. He was about all I did have to stick up to.

He was a good teacher. When I got big enough to trail him around the blacksmith shop, I never got a lickin and I never got swore at there. I got my lickins outdoors when I got into mischief. But in the shop I didn't get into mischief. There were too many tools in there. Chisels and planes and stuff like that where a young kid could get damned hurt. The first thing we got told was, "Be careful." That was all the training we ever got, just watching him work.

Wood will probably last the longest of anything with water running in it. I've taken up pump logs to put in new ones and by gee whiz they'd be wore right through on the bottom where the water had run through till it had wore the wood out. I wouldn't be surprised if they'd last forty years if they were put down in the ground solid. In fact, I've got one up at the shop that's around a hundred years old.

I guess they're about the only pipe that you could manufacture on your own. I won't say that I was at the beginning of it, because I wasn't. It was a long ways back behind me that they were boring logs. But as long as anybody wants to have that work done, I will be available practically any time that they want a demonstration.

Wilma Farman

ONE-ROOM-SCHOOL TEACHER

Lyndonville, Vermont
Born: 1917

➤➤➤➤➤➤➤➤➤➤➤➤➤➤➤➤➤ ⊛ ◄◄◄◄◄◄◄◄◄◄◄◄◄◄◄◄◄◄◄◄

THE ONE-ROOM SCHOOL IS as much a part of American mythology as the covered wagon, the woodshed, and the old two-holer. It would come as a great surprise to most people to learn that some children *still* walk to tiny rural schools where the tradition survives in all its glory. But how good is the one-room school for preparing children for the complex world of the eighties? Everyone will have a different point of view, depending on his or her own experience.

Wilma Farman taught in one-room schoolhouses for forty-two years. She definitely believes that kids do best in that setting. The individual attention, customized lessons, and social virtues of the little red school-house are never obsolete, she says. When she retired recently after teaching thirty years at the Squabble Hollow School, she was teaching the children of parents who themselves had been her students. Mrs. Farman demurs, however, from the recurrent debate over getting back to the basics. "We never lost the basics," she says.

Priorities and gumption are perhaps the central issues in education. This is just as true today as when Dorothy Canfield Fisher wrote *Memories of Arlington, Vermont* about a time long ago when Arlington's covered bridges badly needed repair. The town meeting had to choose between them and the eductional future of the children. Mrs. Fisher sensitively described a town where the future won out over immediate convenience. The isolation of those Vermont farm communities is hard to imagine today. Many of Wilma Farman's families had no radios—never mind TV—and never went out to the movies. As a result, children and their interests were "altogether different."

Wilma Farman's classic rural school was part of a farm society that has changed almost beyond recognition in most of Vermont. One of the basics she was lucky to have was active community participation. Mothers cooked school lunches. Fathers skirted the building for winter and did janitorial work. Parents and teacher got to know each other.

Television has brought the outside world into each child's life. The influence of a national peer group culture has grown as the influence of the family, especially with two working parents, has declined.

To hark back to such a different time for solutions to today's educational crisis may be more romantic than practical. At its best, however, the old tradition of community involvement and caring is never obsolete.

And what of the central figure in the one-room school tableau? Wilma Farman, born in 1917 near Victory Bog, attended a three-room school at Lyndon, Vermont. As a child, this good-natured woman played at being a teacher, at first with her dolls, and later with the boys' ball team. She says that she knew she wanted to be a teacher as soon as she first attended school. During the great Vermont flood of 1928, she cried when classes were cancelled. Even the texture of a teacher's dress passing Wilma's desk was inspirational.

A wartime desk job in Springfield did not lure her away from teaching for long, despite such 1940s school burdens as eight grades together, no teaching assistants, and the social isolation of meeting only parents and the school's superintendent. "There wasn't any special thing I liked best," she says. "I just loved it all."

Squabble Hollow parents have fought off three efforts to close their school. Its scholars still look much like those in the accompanying photo. They are not the great squabblers you might expect from the name Squabble Hollow, which derives from a fight over a pudding.

The one-room school should not be left to mythology and the history books. In some places it continues to thrive and to produce its different kind of person. Dorothy Canfield Fisher wrote about people coming up through such schools "as members of working groups small enough in number to have something of the old town-meeting quality." She said that those boys and girls "were saturated to the marrow of their bones by constant contact with the feelings of communal responsibility for understanding the workings of local institutions and for keeping them working."

To the extent that Vermont's rural schools really did foster community responsibility, their example should be treasured by parents and citizens everywhere.

I went to a three-room school. We used to go in at night and help the first grade teacher. She'd give us a little old stubby crayon she'd been going to throw away and she'd let us correct papers.

From the time I started attending school, my main goal was to be a teacher. I had to work really hard at it because I came from a poor family. I used to go to the mountains to work in the summer for four dollars a week plus whatever tips I could get. I saved every penny so I could go to normal school.

When I was eleven or twelve, I lived on a street with all boys. They'd want me to play baseball because they'd need one more. But if I played baseball with them, they would have to play school with me. I had a little book called *The Harp of God*; I think some religious people had left it at our door. And I had some old pencils I'd acquired from my teacher. That's the equipment I had for my school of boys.

We had an unused barn at our place where the boys would come to play school with me. I would get them to spell words and do arithmetic. I'd tell em a story and make them be quiet. They, of course, would devil around and I'd punish em like the teacher did. I'd grab em by the collar and set em down. [*Laughter.*] When I look back and think! But that was the beginning. I'd do anything I could toward teaching. I'd play school with my dolls.

What the teachers did I wanted to do. I was inspired by the way they did things and by the clothes they wore. For instance, I had one teacher who had a black onyx ring with a diamond in it. I always wanted a black onyx ring.

Back in the days when I went to school if the teacher whipped by our desks and we got a feel of her dress's material, we thought that was a tremendous thing. Kids when I was teaching even asked me where I got my dresses and how much they cost. Back when I went to school, we didn't do those things.

I had a teacher who had little pinch-nosed glasses. She'd read, then she'd take those glasses off. I thought that was clever. My mother always wore her hair in a pug. She had these long wire hairpins and every little while I'd snitch one of those and bend it up so it would flip around and I could pinch it on my nose and have pinch-nosed glasses like Miss Orcutt did.

When I began teaching, I had a superintendent who inspired me. Though I had done practice teaching at the Mosquito School, my first rural school at Walden Heights was where I got my good start. Superintendent John Holden used to come out from Danville once a month and sometimes oftener.

I had a group of boys I didn't know how to teach to read. They weren't on a level with the rest, so John Holden came out specially to observe them. Then he went back to his office and brought out some books. Instead of saying "You do this and you do that," he said, "Would you like me to introduce these books to the boys?" Which was fabulous. I sat and watched him. He did so many nice things and had so many nice ideas. He knew all the children's names and if he were there at recess time, he would go out and play with them. I thought that was just great because I always went out to play with the children, too.

Mr. Holden did so many nice things that he made it fun. Then I thought, "Oh dear, this is for me!"

Oh, I was busy! I didn't have any spare moments but it was really exciting because I knew what was going on in every grade. I think the greatest number of students I had was twenty eight and the smallest number twelve. With the twelve I could do just oodles and oodles. By that time I had quite a lot of experience. It takes a lot of experience. This doesn't come about overnight.

In the beginning, we had a state course of study that everybody in Vermont, whether you were a rural or a graded school, abided by. For instance, I think in second grade you always taught a farm unit. You did a unit on Vermont and the New England states and so forth. Then as time went on we combined units to include more than one grade.

It worked very well to have the older children help the younger ones. For instance, if when we went sliding on the hills in winter there was a little one who couldn't pull his sled back up the hill, one of the older ones would pull it right along for him. It's more like a big family. Or someone whose work is finished will ask if he can help Tommy with his multiplication tables and they go off in a corner somewhere to do it. We'd have several things going on at once in the schoolroom.

A one-room school is the same as an open classroom, but we didn't call it that. There's no place better than a one-room school for real teaching experience because you get to see everything in every grade.

Older ones don't beat up younger ones when they're brought up together like that. They might, if you have a large group and the older ones don't have anything to do. But where they all have to mingle in together, there aren't that many older ones — maybe three or four — and they're perfectly willing to join in with the younger ones.

When you work them into one big family, they learn to have respect for each other.

We did something different every morning. Monday we'd have a planning period of the things we hoped to accomplish during the week. Tuesday mornings we had a little newscast. One of the boys attached a tin can to an iron rod for a microphone; we probably used that microphone for twenty-five years. Everybody would tell a piece of local or national news. The little people could tell anything they thought was news. For instance, maybe their father's choice cow had a heifer calf. Or maybe grandpa had gone to Montpelier. We didn't expect them to have big newsy things. Then on Friday mornings we danced.

We weren't tied down to fifteen minutes for this and fifteen minutes for that. What I didn't get done today I figured I'd pick up tomorrow and go on from there. Also, some of them were perfectly willing to stay after school or stay in at lunch to take extra time.

There weren't very many cars but we took our spring vacation when the mud got so deep you couldn't get through with a car. We'd just call the superintendent and say, "The mud's too deep, so we're going to start our vacation."

The good people who lived right there and who are still living right there were the ones I never had any problems with. Sometimes someone would move in and fit in nicely. But once in awhile somebody would act like a big bully because he'd come from a big school. Then there were children who had had a hot lunch program in a lunchroom and all that and they'd look around and they just couldn't understand.

I noticed that when someone would move in there wasn't the same feeling toward that child; it was sort of like, "You're an outsider."

Our children were more able to cope with questions. They'd discuss em with each other and they would be busy.

We had a cat we raised at school from a kitten. One of the girls took it home during the summer and brought it back in the fall. Then it was taken sick and died and they felt really bad.

Some of the children thought I was strict, but they all remember the good times we had. They all chipped in and bought me a skidoo suit for sliding the year skidoo suits first came out; I was the only one in school who didn't have one. One of the families was very poor and couldn't afford to put in any money, but the mother knitted me a pair of mittens, which was very, very nice.

One year I had a girl in the eighth grade and I had had her all eight years and I just couldn't see how I could go back to school another year without that girl. Graduation night I cried. We usually had a school director or a minister or somebody come to present the diplomas but she insisted that *I* present her the diploma not somebody from outside.

But she went on, and the next year someone just stepped in where she'd been and things went on just the same.

Many former students call or come to see me. I think it pleases any teacher to have pupils do that, even though they remind you of some of the things you've done — like spanking them — which you've forgotten. Anyway, it does me good. When they had my retirement party, a boy called me from California.

Our pupils took turns doing the duties like cleaning the blackboards and sweeping the floor and cleaning the toilet and dusting and taking care of the bookcases. But if we needed any outside help, like if the water froze, we'd call one of the fathers up. The fathers saved us a lot of money. They always put the paper around the foundation of the building to make it warmer for winter. They always shoveled the snow off the roof. In fact, they painted the school building, too.

In the early days parents didn't have any time to get involved. Many of them never came to visit school except when we had a program. Like Halloween, usually a box supper. At Christmastime we went all out and had a real nice program. And the grammies and the grandpas and the aunts and the uncles and the little preschoolers all came.

We tried to make the school a social center because there wasn't much socializing back in the good old days. I remember having card parties at the Mosquito School. One of the fathers would hitch up his team of horses and put some hay in the bottom of the sled and put blankets over it. He'd stop along the way and pick up all the people.

Teachers should participate in community affairs to get to know the parents. I think you can do a much better job if you know the type of home a child comes from. I liked to know the parents. Many times they would call and say, "Scott's off to a bad start this morning. If he has a bad day, you'll know it's something that's happened here at home." Or, "So-and-so was sick all night but decided she wanted to go to school. I've let her go, but if she's sick during the day, call me."

When I first started teaching, the kids all came from farm homes and they brought their own hot lunches. Sometimes they brought em in a little jar. Mashed potatoes or maybe soup. I had a big old canner I put on top of the wood stove to heat the jars. That was our hot lunch program.

Understand that I taught in the days when we had the little outhouse and the wood stove.

Over at Walden Heights, the parents would take turns cooking up something. Maybe one day a parent would bring in a hot bottle of soup. What I liked the best were the hot johnnycakes an old lady would bring in in big pans. Those children liked everything, particularly if it was something Mrs. Burbank or Mrs. Guillen made.

When I started having the children of parents I'd taught, I sometimes thought it was good because those parents would say, "Now, when you go to school, Mrs. Farman won't let you do that." But sometimes those kids were afraid of me before they got there.

Their parents just laughed and thought it was a joke, but the kids were all prepared when they came. The parents knew me and I knew them and, well, it was really great.

They have saved their Squabble Hollow School three times from being closed. Some of those people's parents went to school there and they realize the fun and the value of the closeness that they have with the school.

We never lost the basics. I don't see how anyone can teach school and not use the basics. This has puzzled me. It's the same with values. Well, how can you teach without values? Isn't there a value on almost everything you do? These things really amaze me.

Toward the end of my teaching, we had a phys ed teacher, a music teacher, and an art teacher who came in. I can't see that we lacked anything. Back in the good old days, we had none of those. And the poor children . . . If they had a teacher they didn't like, it was difficult. Particularly if the poor things had to have the same teacher eight years, and many of my students did have me for all eight years.

I think it's a sad thing that those who could have the opportunity to go to one-room schools can't because the schools have been phased out. In several places it would have been much cheaper to have kept the one-room school and to have paid the teacher rather than bus the children. In the beginning most of those children walked to school.

I realized that not all children can go to one-room schools because of the cities and so forth. But for those who can . . . Personally I think the one-room school is the thing. It's almost one-to-one. The teacher is busy, but she knows every child and she knows every parent. It's not the building that counts; it's what you have in the building.

I'd look forward to it all again. I just loved it.

Ernest Flanders

INVENTOR

Springfield, Vermont
Born: 1895

➤➤➤➤➤➤➤➤➤➤➤➤➤➤➤➤ ✳ ◄◄◄◄◄◄◄◄◄◄◄◄◄◄◄◄◄◄◄

SPRINGFIELD INVENTOR ERNEST FLANDERS SAYS that he "never wanted a job where everybody knew the answers." Instead, he says, he thrived as a troubleshooter for stuff that had never been done before. Today, Vermont needs his Yankee ingenuity more than ever.

The ingenious mechanic, that classic figure of nineteenth-century American folklore, has fallen on hard times. Not only is American technological supremacy a thing of the past in everyday items such as automobiles and typewriters but the inventor as hero needs to be reinvented. Ernest Flanders is such a hero.

The late Senator Ralph Flanders was Ernest's brother and mentor. He was the courageous Vermont Republican who first called for the censure of Joe McCarthy in the U.S. Senate and who earlier had risen rapidly in Springfield's Jones & Lamson Machine Company—marrying the owner's daughter—to create important inventions in the field of precision grinding. In their engineering work, Ralph and Ernest Flanders complemented each other's strengths. "Whenever he designed something new or put something new on the market," Ernest says of his brother, "he always expected me to be able to meet any situation that might arise. So as I got more experience, I was closely associated with him and with others in the industry who were involved with things they couldn't understand and hoped somebody would give em an answer for."

In 1947, at the beginning of the jet aircraft era, General Electric could produce only one engine turbine blade an hour because of the complexity of the grinding requirements. GE ordered five new grinding machines from Jones & Lamson on the basis of a theoretical discussion with the Flanders brothers, who promised that each as-yet-undesigned grinder would produce twenty blades an hour. Since each jet needed ninety-six blades, this radical breakthrough in productivity was a real coup. When Jones & Lamson president Ralph Flanders received the prestigious Edward Longstreth Medal of Merit for achievement in engineering, he insisted on sharing it with Ernest, who was then manager of the Grinding Division.

The Flanders' years in Springfield epitomized Yankee ingenuity at its best. But recently distant corporate forces have put Vermont's machine tool industry on the skids. So far Springfield business leaders have been unsuccessful at buying back the industrial heart of their town from its conglomerate owners. This problem extends far beyond Springfield and Vermont. Nowadays the Northeast's industrial states are often labeled the Rust Belt, in comparison to the dynamic Sun Belt states. But idle factories, unemployed workers, and paralyzed towns are not inevitable, says Ernest Flanders. The important thing to remember is that people's brains haven't rusted. With the right kind of education, leadership, and community involvement, Yankee ingenuity could once again set new standards in productivity and invention.

I asked Ernest Flanders about Japan's current reputation for superiority in the type of precision engineering for which he was famous. "That bothers me. I regret that," he said. "Number one, we have to have people like my brother to conceive the methods. Then we need to have somebody on hand to solve the problems and not just leave em to Tom, Dick, and Harry and let come what will."

Both Ernest and his brother were perfectionists. Their father was a self-taught mechanic, who designed and built some woodworking equipment but who never had a job commensurate with his abilities. Nevertheless, his example of perfectionism stayed with his sons. "He encouraged me to do everything right," says Ernest. "In working with him, I was always looking to do the best I could. To make a quality job of whatever I did. My father, no matter what *he* did, it *had* to be right.

"He'd take the time to make it right."

I think it was very fortunate in my makeup because I didn't have a jealous nature. I was interested in what I was doing and if somebody else was involved with it, that was all right with me. My brother, Ralph Flanders, was the brains of the family. The family was in tough shape when he was growing up; he went into Brown and Sharp and became a machinist and from there went out into industry.

When I came along fifteen years later, he put me in Norton Company and made me a machinist. They built grinding wheels and grinding machinery in Worcester, Massachusetts. So I had good training.

Ralph Flanders (left) and Ernest Flanders (right)

In World War I, not many people had the wide range of training I had. I left engineering school and went to work for the company building the early Hispano-Suiza airplanes. They didn't keep me in the shop long but sent me out in the field to check on what was happening there. I covered the whole of western New York to work on problems. I was pretty busy doing things that interested me. It was an interesting couple of years. I married when I was out there.

My brother, who was manager of Jones & Lamson, said that he wanted me to come here because my mother and father were getting very old. Also, because from what he'd seen of me, he thought that I could be a help to him and the plant.

So in 1920 I moved to Springfield. They were hard times. There wasn't much business.

When things picked up and we began to build for growing aeronautics companies and automotive companies, they put me on the road going where there were troubles and finding answers to them.

The way I worked into it was that my brother would design something and then he'd get involved in something else. Jones & Lamson had quite a wide variety of machines; their original product was a turret lathe. One time they wanted to develop something that was not always mounted in a chuck on the spindle. And my brother did it. Then they wanted to have something that would turn a centered piece. There used to be problems of dimensioning and of duplication. In his final years, my brother developed a machine that was used by the aeronautics industry for many of their very important parts. For instance, there was a gas turbine that had to be made with an inside tolerance of two tenths of a thousand (.0002). I worked on that problem for some little time and was able to solve it. We made a big business of supplying machines just on that one job.

Another job involved the base of a turbine fan in which there were grooves on either side that had to be an exact distance apart.

The turbine problem was one of the closest problems in dimensioning that I know of. It came just at a time when the standard engine was not good enough for a plane. This led to the gas turbine, which is probably used today more than any other engine.

You are familiar with putting high pressure on turbine blades. They develop a lot of power and are very efficient. In this particular instance you had to direct not water but gas and to get the gas exploding at the time it was hitting the rotating member. It had to be *dead right*. We had to true the grinding wheel to the shape we wanted with an allowance of only a tenth and a half a thousandth (.00015). To do that I eventually worked up an idea of using a rotating member with diamonds in it. The whole surface was covered with diamonds; up until that time we could only use one diamond. We found many opportunities to use this new type of rotating diamond wheel dressing to change the pattern of production in many fields.

I used to do a lot of work between two and four in the morning in bed. I'd think about what would make it possible for us to go on the way we intended to. The hours from half past one in the morning till four were very important hours for me. Go to bed and go to sleep. Wake up at half past one and go to thinking. I knew that I would not do my best thinking at the end of the day when I was tired but sometime between half past one and four or five o'clock.

In the early years that I was here, my brother was the chief engineer. Later he was president of the company.

My brother spent an awful lot of time thinking. And he encouraged me. We worked very well together. I'd report to him. I found it convenient and much to his liking to tell him any troubles I was having and what I was doing about em. And what I thought the future would bring for us. He liked to have me work with him on his problems. I know I must have done him a lot of good in his later years because it gave him time to involve himself in some other matters, like politics.

Whenever I saw him, I'd tell him what I was doing. In the shop or sometimes we might be mountain climbing. He used to love to climb mountains and so did I. I'd talk about some of the problems I was focusing on and what I wanted to do about em. From my point of view it was important that there be somebody along the line somewhere who could understand the problems and would appreciate the solutions.

The average man who went into the shop was interested in getting a job and making so much money an hour. My salary was never so important to me that I didn't take far more pleasure in developing an idea than in the money I made. And I never was a highly paid individual. I got enough to live on.

My brother was very clever in handling problems. He found that I had something he could use and he used it. I never had any words of irritation from him all my life. He was always very good to me.

As I look back over the years, I congratulate myself on the work and the way it was accomplished.

William Godfrey

AUCTIONEER

Ely, Vermont
Born: 1900

➤➤➤➤➤➤➤➤➤➤➤➤➤➤➤➤ ⊛ ◄◄◄◄◄◄◄◄◄◄◄◄◄◄◄◄◄◄

BILL GODFREY IS ABOUT AS CLOSE to my ideal picture of a Vermonter as any-body I ever met. Naturally, my Vermonter would be a farmer; and Bill Godfrey was, having grown up on his parents' place—where he still lives—near Lake Fairlee. I'd want him to know something about sugaring and Bill has been making sugar from the time he was "big enough to wal-low through the snow to gather sap." I'd want my man to know something about livestock, too. And Bill has auctioned off more horses and cattle than any other living Vermonter.

The right fella for my picture would be neighborly. That's Bill all right. Much of the produce from his acre-sized vegetable patch goes to his less active friends. And when I visited him one sunny January day, he was cooking a chicken dinner to take to a shut-in neighbor.

My composite Vermonter would be a hard worker who combined fru-gality for himself with fairness and generosity toward his customers. In short, someone for whom honesty means not just the letter of the law. This truly is one of the most remarkable things about Bill Godfrey. He has not exacted the contemporary last pound of bottom-line flesh in any of his three careers—sugarmaker, undertaker, or auctioneer.

A common un-Godfrey way to increase profit in the first of Bill's three professions is to add cheap cane syrup to maple sugar candy. (That's what gives it those sparkling flakes *and* inferior taste.) As for the funeral business, the price of someone's moving into that hole in the ground is likely to exceed the mortgage on his house. Unless Bill Godfrey is the undertaker: He is still actively burying friends and strangers alike at prices that reflect a by-gone era. He even makes up wooden cremation caskets from lumber milled from his own woodlot in order to save money. (No wonder he's not loved by the rest of the bereavement business.) When it comes to auc-tioneering, the smart operator will charge a percentage of the take, employ shills in the crowd to jack up the bids, and lay down an incomprehensible patter to distance himself from the rubes out front.

But not William Godfrey.

His must have been a hard life, standing outside in the elements all day and working through the night with dead bodies. But Bill Godfrey fits another of my requisites for the ideal Vermonter: He has a wonderful sense of humor. In fact, next to his incomparable accent, humor is the most charming thing about him. He is always ready to tell or enjoy a good old-fashioned Vermont story. He has that understated humor, too, such as when he explains his feelings about burying old friends: "Somebody's got to get used to doctors' errors."

Imagine for a moment what it was like at one of his auctions. The big day arrives. The colorful auction bills have been posted in surrounding country stores and along the roads. People dribble up to the farm from the shunpikes and byways and descend on the items to be sold. Old friends greet the auctioneer, who cracks a joke about the day ahead. The dapper man is attired in a straw hat; a bow tie; an impeccably starched button-down shirt; a vest, with pocket watch; black lace-up boots; and perhaps, as protection against manure, a pair of overalls. His regular cashier and clerk arrive. Bill Godfrey mounts his worn auction block in the barn entrance. All is ready. Using a no-nuisance microphone, he begins to state the terms of sale.

Unfortunately, nowadays the informal style of the old country auction is largely a thing of the past. As one admirer put it, "Godfrey gives the crowd the feeling that he is a conspirator in the dangerous, daredevil process of bidding, whereas the no-nonsense commercial mood created by many younger auctioneers subtly alienates the audience."

I am sorry that the state of Vermont does not have the Japanese government's system of naming certain individuals as living national treasures, because Bill Godfrey is a living state treasure.

I think the best way to end this chapter is with some authentic Bill Godfrey auctioneering.

Any bidders?

I auctioneered fifty-six years. Some years I did as high as sixty-three auctions. All kinds of auctions. Everything. Antiques. Settling estates. Cattle auctions.

I started in in 1924 up to Wells River. Oh, I used to sell for all the old cattle and horse jockeys there. Nate Nutter, Ote Lisbon, and Ote Smith. A dozen dealers. Horse jockeys trade horses all the time—the same as these automobile dealers trade cars.

I didn't do that darned crazy stuff they do nowadays where you can't understand a word they say. I talked so they could understand what I was talking about. [*Laughter.*] Oh, I went fast enough. I've made a thousand sales in a day, settling an estate. Household goods.

When I first began auctioneering, you'd have a farm auction, an all-day sale, and they always fed the whole crowd. They'd have crackers and cheese put up in paper bags and if it was a good auction, lotsa times they'd put in two or three Mary Anne ginger cookies. They'd have a wash boiler on the stove with the coffee brewing in it. Every man had a tin cup on his suspenders or his belt and they went around in line at noon to get that coffee and the bags of St. Johnsbury or White River crackers and three or four chunks of cheese. At a good auction like that, the man used to buy a whole cheese and the women folks'd be putting it up in the morning in the bags when you went to the auction.

Well, there'd be some of these old fellas'd be afraid they weren't getting their money's worth so they'd go around the line two or three times and stick the bags in their pockets. Well, along half past three or four we'd get about ready to sell the cattle and while we were waiting for them to come into the ring those old fellas'd begin to pull out them bags and try to bite them crackers. Of course, the coffee was gone then and their teeth weren't too good. [*Laughter.*] It was funny seeing them try to bite those crackers!

The auction was a lot of people's entertainment. It didn't cost em anything, only what they spent for the stuff they bought. That's all. And they got a free lunch from the farmer. We had good times at auctions right up till I quit selling. The folks that go to auctions, they won't let the other fella have it—no matter what the price is. I saw one old fella who got sore at another man cause he'd bid against him. God, he was gonna knock him down.

Sometimes I'd be selling a sofa or something like that and there'd be a man and a girl bidding on it. I'd say to the fella—I'd be trying to get more money out of him—I'd say, "Are you gonna let a woman trim ya for five dollars?" And he'd say, "Yup." I'd say, "Well, now I wouldn't do that." I said, "You'd pay a doctor or a lawyer good money for advice but I ain't gonna charge ya anything for advice. If I were you, I wouldn't let that girl have it. I'd buy that sofa and then I'd invite the girl over to supper some night and I'd get acquainted with her and the sofa, too, at the same time."

In some ways the old days were better. Years ago you just had the horse and buggy or sleigh. But, of course, you can cover more territory with the automobile. One time to an auction down in Thetford here there was a fella had a pair of mules hitched on a four-wheel wagon. He hitched em up near a pigpen but the pigs were asleep when he tied the mules there to a fence. Well, all at once we heard the boards crash up above. The pigs had come out and those mules were scairt and they broke away and come down through the crowd. Everybody grabbed for em and stopped em. Just one man was hurt a little.

The farmer always gave a warm dinner in the house to the auctioneer, the cashier, and the clerk, and some of the best buyers. Then for the last twenty-five years we didn't get a warm dinner. We got [*disgustedly*] hot dogs and hamburgers. Hot dogs and hamburgers! Oh, back then we didn't get so much money, but we did get a warm dinner.

The last warm dinner Dan Perry and I had was at a big auction over at East Randolph. God, they put on a regular Thanksgiving. They had roast chicken, the devil and all. Yeah, they had all the pies and cakes and everything to go with it.

Dan Perry was an older man. He used to have the Ford business over in Barre. In the forties his boy went in the service and he called me up to see if I could help him out.

He was a good auctioneer. Not one of those can't-understand-a-word-they-say types. Just a regular, good, straight-talking man. He was a good, honest fella, too.

There's quite a lot of em that aren't too honest. [*Laughter.*] A cracked dish or something else—they'd put their thumb over it. Their sales are all final. If you buy something, it's yours. You couldn't bring it back if you found a crack in it.

Sometimes they'd sell a darned balky horse. They used to have signs up on the sales table at Wells River, "Every Horse Guaranteed." The next sign would read, "All Guarantees Expire at 4 P.M. on the Date of Sale." They knew buyers wouldn't get home with em, so that's the way they got by with that. [*Laughter.*]

Sometimes a horse would have the heaves or something and they'd load em up with shot in their stomach. Of course, the horse lived until the shot wore through its stomach. Then it just dropped dead on em somewhere. But nobody would know how long that shot had been in there.

Oh, they had a lot of tricks, the same as car dealers do.

Dan Perry was a good auctioneer. We'd swap off. He'd sell an article and then I'd sell an article. We'd do that all day long. That way it'd give us a rest break in between.

He used to tell stories, same as I did. If bidding was slow, we used to tell stories to get em started. We'd tell anything to get the crowd laughing.

For instance, back in the wartime when Roosevelt was president there was a young fella got a job selling war bonds down around Boston. And he warn't having too good luck. They told him all the money was up in Vermont and New Hampshire cause them fellas up there were getting three dollars a hundred for their milk. So that's the place he wanted to go. He told his wife, "Tomorrow morning I'm leaving for Vermont. I'll come back loaded tomorrow night."

The first farmhouse he stopped at there was an old lady out sweeping the porch. The fella says, "Is the man of the house around?"

She says, "Yes, he's out in the barn cleaning the stables."

He says, "Can I go out and talk to him?"

She say, "All you want to, but you'll have to speak pretty loud 'cause he's kinda deaf."

So he goes out to the barn with his briefcase and things and the old man was there. He says to the old man, "I'm a bond salesman."

And the old man says, "What of it?"

He says, "Hadn't ya heard there's a war goin on?"

The old man just shook his head.

He says, "Hadn't ya heard about Pearl Harbor?"

"Oh, I never heard nothing bad about her. She's a good girl as far as I know. She lives up the road here a couple of miles," he says.

He says, "You must have heard about Winston Churchill?"

The old man just shook his head.

He says, "You must have heard about President Roosevelt?"

And the old man just shook his head.

So the bond salesman picked up his briefcase and went down and got in his car and went off.

The old man went down to the house in a few minutes and his wife said, "Who was that fella?"

He said, "Darned if I know."

"Well," she said, "what did he want?"

He said, "I couldn't make head nor tail to his story. Near as I could make out some fella name of Roosevelt had got Pearl Harbor in trouble over on Church Hill and he wanted me to go bonds for her and I'll be damned if I will." [*Laughter.*]

You could get a lot more money for bids after telling a story. You'd get some good bidding after these stories and folks'd come around and ask ya to tell it again so they could remember it.

One noon there was a minister and his wife who used to come up from Massachusetts. She asked me if I was going to tell some stories. She needed some to tell to her club at their next meeting.

It got to be two o'clock and she said, "Ain't you gonna tell a story?" She set right down in fronta me.

I said, "Well, seein you're a minister's wife, I'll tell a ministerial story today."

Johnny had a great time of saying "by God." He'd catch a fish and he'd tell his mother, "By God, ain't that a good one?" Or he'd have some pie to eat and, "By God, that's good, ma'am."

His mother was trying to break him of saying "by God," so she told him he mustn't say that word. "The minister and his wife are coming up for supper tomorrow night and he doesn't say that word."

Johnny says, "By God, I bet he does."

"Well," she says, "when he gets here we'll ask him."

When the minister got there, she told him what a time she was having trying to break Johnny of saying, "by God." She told him, "I said you never use that word."

And the minister says, "Oh no, Johnny, I never use that word."

Johnny says, "By God, I bet you do."

"Well," the minister says, "I don't bet very often but I'm so sure of myself this time that I'm gonna bet with ya. What do you want to bet?"

And Johnny says, "Do you like apple pie?"

The minister says, "Yes."

"Well," Johnny says, "if I can get my mother to make one, I'll bet you an apple pie that you use that word."

The minister says, "Well you come to church Sunday morning and you set right up in the front pew so you can hear."

So Johnny set there. The sermon was gettin about over and he's beginnin to itch around and finally the minister says, "By God we live, by God we die."

Johnny jumps up and says, "By God, you lose your apple pie." [*Laughter.*]

Ladies and gentlemen, the terms of sale in four letters are C, A, S, H. The cashier is waiting out under the green umbrella in the back. If two people claim the same bid on the same item, we'll put it up again for sale. The sunshine is free.

All right, what'll ya give for this little walnut rocker right here? What'll ya give? It's missing a slat in the seat. Well now, if you sit down with a smile, I'll guarantee you'll get up with a stare.

All right, what'll you give? Ten dollars, he says on the corner.

He'll come to it. Fifteen dollars.

Yup. Seventeen. We've got it. Eighteen. Now the twenty. Can I hear thirty?

Thirty. Yeah, you'll pay the five. Yuh, thirty-five. Two and a half. Can I hear the two and a half?

Once, twice. Sold for thirty-five dollars to the gentleman over there in the straw hat.

Chester "Chet" Grimes

HORSE LOGGER AND STORYTELLER

Lyndonville, Vermont
Born: 1905

➤➤➤➤➤➤➤➤➤➤➤➤➤➤➤➤➤ ⊛ ◄◄◄◄◄◄◄◄◄◄◄◄◄◄◄◄◄◄◄

A FEW YEARS AGO A SUBJECT of fashionable conversation was truckers' CB language. Even people who did not want to know were soon aware that *handle* could mean nickname and that *Smoky* was not the handle of a Forest Service bear. While the fad lasted, bumper stickers proliferated ("You don't need a CB to talk to Jesus") and teamsters were idolized as knights of the road. What, I wonder, would CBers have thought if they had met my favorite teamster, Chet Grimes, a man so unimpressed by technology that he never made the switch from horse teams to motor vehicles?

In northern Vermont horse logging has never entirely died out. But even among those who still skid with the big draft horses, Chet Grimes is an anachronism. "I put more money into horses than I ever did into myself," he says. "It always kept me poor but I don't regret a mite of it."

A recent documentary recognized Chet Grimes as a great spokesman for old-time horse logging. The man simply lives and breathes horses. Despite his poor health, he scrupulously cares for four enormous hayburners, whose appetites bite heavily into his minuscule Social Security check. Poor as church mice, Chet and his companion Helen Hutchinson have neither car nor electricity nor indoor plumbing. Yet the welfare of those four huge pets definitely comes first.

There are more horses today in Vermont than at any time since the introduction of the automobile. I wish that today's breeders and owners could meet Chet Grimes and hear his stories about his heroes, the old horse teamsters, and learn his secrets for keeping a team "as fat as seals."

As my contribution to the revival of a noble animal, I am offering here four classic Chet Grimes stories: meeting a famous liar; pulling to win at the county fair; draying logs off a steep mountainside; and learning the right way to harness a log skidding team.

But first Chet has something to say about the old teamsters he learned from as a boy. Sit back and listen to a great country storyteller, who always starts off, "Now, mister, I'm going to tell ya something . . ."

There were a lot of old horse teamsters I looked up to. Marshall Slumham was one. A regular old teamster. It's all he ever done. When I was eight, nine, ten years old, every time I got a chance I would go with Marshall cause I liked to see him handle the horses. I rode miles and miles with him on the team.

He was just a good everyday regular old Vermonter. He had a family and worked for a living. Driving team back then was like driving trucks now. A lot of people had teams and they hired a man to drive em.

Marshall Slumham was an awful good teamster. He knew how to handle a horse, how to harness one, and he knew what they ought to do. You know, there's any amount of em's got horses today who don't know what a horse should do. They think he should work twelve hours a day, then throw him in the barn, toss him a lift of hay and a little water, and that's it. They didn't used to take care of the horses like that.

Chet Grimes

Them old fellas used to take good care of their horses. They cleaned em off, kept em bedded and blanketed in winter. And they took care of em. That's what kept the team going. If something serious didn't happen, they'd have a team for ten, fifteen years.

Of course, we had *logs* back then. I mean eighteen, twenty, twenty-four inches on the stump. And just as straight as a bean pole.

One time Marshall had twenty-eight hundred feet on a double set of narrow gauge sleds and a good pair of mares pulling. He run four bridle chains—some people call em sled runner chains—to slow the sleds. And I rode down with him on that load of logs. Don't worry, boy, I'll never forget it!

He was a teamster. He never talked to them horses as loud as I'm talking to you. Never. Now, he'd made em mind somewhere; they knew him. He could take them right out here and say to one of em—their names were Bess and Beauty—and he'd say, Bess, step ahead two feet. And she'd go just exactly two foot. I guarantee you could've measured it with a rule.

MEETING A FAMOUS LIAR

One time we were up on East Hill with the four horses honing the road. One team was picking up sod and stones and filling in holes with em. And this Jimmy Peters come by.

Oh, he was an awful liar. Them Peterses was quite a rig anyway. Everybody knew he was an awful liar. He had his horse and buggy and was driving right along with a little switch in his hand. Somebody said to him, "C'mon, Jimmy, and tell us a lie."

"God," he said, "I can't. A man was on his barn roof shingling and fell off and broke his leg and I'm headed for the doctor."

Jimmy struck the horse with his switch and away down the road he went. Well, we knew that fella well. We'd been honing by there and picking sod and he'd been on the roof shingling. Well we set down to dinner and Gerry, the road commissioner, said, "Let's go back over and see if there's anything we can do to help him." We all piled in my wagon, four or five of us, and we drove back over there.

And here set the old man on his steps smoking his pipe, just as nice as a pin. There warn't nothing wrong with him atall. He hadn't fell and broke his leg.

Peters said he didn't have time to tell us a lie but when we got over there that old man hadn't fell and broke his leg at all.

PULLING TO WIN AT THE COUNTY FAIR

The last time I pulled in that ring up there at the Barton fair-grounds I drove Gordon Thompson's team. I was seventy-two years old. Well, I was hanging around there and Gordon wanted me to drive his little chestnut horse. That was an awful miserable horse to hitch on the board.

And it was the 32 class is what it was. He brought em up and handed me the lines.

I said, "I'll tell ya one thing, Gordon, I'm gonna beat you and Raleigh True."

He said, "That'll be the day. You'll be behind us three places. Don't worry."

I didn't care about beating anybody else. I just wanted to beat Gordon 'cause he'd had the chestnut in the 30 class before that and then he put him with Jim and made a 32 team. Then he brought his good 32 team in, too, and was going to take the whole contest.

Well, I figured I had two pretty good evener hitchers. I said, "Boys, when we drive in, I don't give a damn how them horses be. You drop that hook on when I say drop er, mister. Don't pull. We ain't placing them. We'll let them place themselves."

That little chestnut was a rotten little puke to hitch. 'Cause, I'll tell ya, he'd find out what you was doin and then he'd move his hind end and crowd right out. I said to the boys, "I see how he's working and we'll fool him."

They said, "What are you going to do?"

I said, "I'll go in one way one time and another way the next and he won't know where to go."

So that's what I done. The boat sat like this—he was the nigh horse—and I'd come down around and swing right tight to the boat and say, "Drop her boys." And we never straightened up nor tried to hitch on square or nuthin. He was hitched before he knew it, see. I kept right up next to the rail and went right out with it. Next time I'd go the other way.

I didn't win the class, but I beat them two fellas that I wanted to beat. Well, mister, I stayed till I drawed three load more'n Gordon and three load more'n Raleigh and beat them both with that team.

Raleigh said, "You old bastard." [*Laughter.*]

Of course, we was just raisin the devil, that's all. Nobody was mad or nuthin. We had a lot of fun.

DRAYING LOGS OFF A STEEP MOUNTAINSIDE

I've logged all my life off some awful steep mountains.

Do you know where the old asbestos mine is over to Eden? What they call the New England Mine? Well, I've logged off'n that. And, mister, I'll tell ya quite a little story about it.

I had a pair of mares that weighed about twenty-eight hundred and I'd worked em about two years together. We'd been up there draying off pulp, drawing it off the mountain behind a sled. It got about the last of March and eight to ten cords were still up there. The boss, Matty Thomas, came down to see me. He said, "Would you go up and get that pulp if I went and helped you?"

I said, "Gee, I don't know if we can get up that road now or not, but I'll try it."

The snow was deeper'n hell on that mountain but twas thawin, ya know, comin spring.

We went up and we got two load one day, two load the next day, and we was after the last load.

Going down, it was so steep that I used to put a cord of wood in a bobsled behind the dray to slow it down. The snow was so soft that the runner chains didn't hold too good. Each runner on the dray was chained with what the old fellas called a bridle chain. It went right around the runner with a rig made on purpose for it.

I said to Matty, "We'll be happy if we get this load off the mountain."

We had a place—I helped build it—between two ledges that was about eight feet deep. We'd filled it with old logs and brush and stones in the fall and then broke a road right over it before the snow came. We got down there and my Ruby mare stepped through a goddamn hole. When she went down, that high-nosed sled—a two-beam sled they call em—cocked up and its pole stuck right in the snow, just like my bent elbow, only upside down.

There we set with that three cord of wood on that punt and with the old mare hung up so that all the parts of her hames were just as tight as a fiddler's bitch.

Matty said, "Cut the tug."

I said, "No, don't cut them new tugs. Let's begin to unbuckle. Then we'll get a stick of that pulp and put it under that bridge beam to brace it."

So I dug a stick of pulp out and Matty reached in under that five-foot-long sled. The front end was cocked up right in the air; the sled pole was stuck in the ground, just like if you took this paper and doubled it over. And with that load of pulp on it right over the horses.

We got it braced so it would stay there. I kept talking to the old mare and she laid right still; they was awful good to mind.

First we got a side strap unbuckled. Then Matty got one tug free. (It goes from the hame to the sled to draw by—traces they call em.)

We got them harnesses all unbuckled and got the horses out. And shoveled a place for em off the road so they could stand.

Matty said, "What in hell are you going to do now with that load of pulp? We'll have to unload it."

I said, "No. Let's dig that pole out and see if it'll set there just a minute." So we dug the pole out and got the neck yokes off'n it, that the horses had been hitched to.

I said, "Let's see if we can tip that pole up. Don't get under the front end of the sled or it'll get ya if that block of wood comes out." That piece of pulp was about four feet long and braced up under there. It just fit in good.

We got the pole up and hitched a chain to what you'd call the dashboard at the front of the sled. "Now," he said, "what are you going to do?"

I said, "We'll pry that goddamn stick out and let that son-of-a-bitch go down the mountain."

And that's what we done. And now, mister, I'm gonna tell ya, it *went* down that mountain.

There was a sharp bend at the bottom. Not an awful sharp one, but sharp enough. They'd logged that off down there and it had grown up in little maples. That load of pulp went right out onto them maples and set right up there off the ground, sled and all.

Matty said, "It's at the foot of the mountain."

"Hell," I said, "let's put the harnesses together." So we got the harnesses back together. I hitched the old mares and drove em down to the sled.

I could just barely reach over to that sled with a chain from the road. But I drawed that load of pulp back onto the road and went down and unloaded it and came back and picked up that bunch we had left behind and dragged that down and piled it up.

And Matty said, "I'm glad that job is done."

LEARNING THE RIGHT WAY TO HARNESS A LOG SKIDDING TEAM

Bub Noyes lived down below here. His name was Carroll but we all called him Bub. He had a pair of ponies up here. He said, "I'm gonna see if I can skid a few of them logs you got cut." Steve Switzer was with him.

Why, they had the damndest time with them ponies. They'd run and yank and jump. They couldn't do nuthin. So they skidded eight or ten logs and quit.

Switzer said to Bub, "You've got to get some different bits on them ponies or you'll never hold em."

I didn't say anything. I just stood there. He said it three or four times. Finally, I said, "How would it be if he made some spreaders and put em up where they ought to be? Don't you think he could drive em then?"

"You can drive em right through the hame like that."

I said, "You Switzer's never could drive a horse. Or a pony either. I'm going to tell you right to your damned head."

Well, Bub left em here. The next morning I got up and I felt goodern hell. I was alright then. I hadn't been sick any to speak of. I was old, seventy-something, but I warn't sick.

I went to the barn, cleaned those ponies, and throwed the harnesses on em. I took those lines and shortened them and riveted em back in and fixed em the way they should be. Then I got a strap and made some spreaders and put em on the hames.

I went to the woods and skidded twenty-two logs. I'd just got done before noon and put em in the barn, when Bub came up and said, "Who skidded the logs?"

I said, "I did, using Mack and Dino."

He said, "You did like hell."

I said, "They're still harnessed in the barn; I didn't know but I'd use em a little drawin out manure this afternoon on my sled."

He said, "I don't believe it."

I said, "OK, Bub, you'll kill me but I'll tell you one thing. If I've ruined your lines, if they ain't as good as they ever was, I'll buy you a new set. But I cut em off and fixed em the way they ought to be. And put some spreaders on them hames. When they've had their grain and water and have stood about an hour, there's some logs up there I want you to skid with em."

Bub went up and they skidded just like a yoke of oxen. They was just as quiet. You could back em up. There was no jumping or balking or nuthin.

"Well, by God," Bub said, "I've learned one thing. That you've got to have things fit if you're ever gonna use em."

Jim King

WOODS COOK

Concord, Vermont
Born: 1890

❯❯❯❯❯❯❯❯❯❯❯❯❯❯❯❯ ✳ ❮❮❮❮❮❮❮❮❮❮❮❮❮❮❮❮

JIM KING WAS BORN IN CONCORD, Vermont and worked in the Northeast Kingdom's logging camps for many years. Beginning as a *cookee* or cook's apprentice, he rose to serve ten years as camp boss. In the rough Paul Bunyan–world of loggers, that was quite a feat. As Jim himself was quick to tell me, he is "a pretty shrewd operator."

Chet Grimes and I went to see him at his spacious Lancaster, New Hampshire home. Despite failing sight and the amputation of both legs, Jim received us heartily and soon fell to dickering with Chet over the price of an old sleigh and some harnesses. They had traded often before for horses and equipment and the talk turned to past deals. Jim emphasized that he had always "kept a good name" and that he had bought and sold fifty farms and woodlots, some more than once, and that he had often had as many as sixty-five horses for sale. Compared to church-mouse-poor Chet, the older man was a country Croesus.

As far as I could tell, age had not slowed Jim King in the slightest. I thought to myself that if every Vermonter were as frugal and sharp as these two old rascals the rest of the country had better watch out. "Oh, I know how to do business," Jim said gleefully. His large garage was jam-packed with household furnishings, horse tack, and anything else that could be bought and sold at a profit. Well, not everything. Not the load of caskets he had once bought for $650 from a failed mortuary and immediately resold for $1,000. "Well, I've done everything. I was in the hospital having my legs amputated and I sold just as much stuff from there as I do here. I know my business. I can puzzle a lot of these fellas on a lot of stuff they don't know about. I know what the law is; I studied it out. I didn't go to school, only to fifth grade, but I can puzzle these folks today. I've operated some!"

The energy that Jim King put into a long life of logging, trading, and living must have been evident early on. At age seventeen, he had as many as 120 men to feed in the logging camp at Victory, Vermont. As his admirer, Chet Grimes, puts it; "He's a corking good hand to do things. He's a real nice fella. If he tells ya something, you can bet it's no lie. He ain't a double-barreled shit-ass, let's put it that way. He's honest; he'll treat you right. If you don't do him right, you won't have to ask the neighbors to find out about it. He'll tell ya right to your face."

I went in there on Labor Day, September 1907. I was seventeen years old. I worked seven days in the woods swamping roads. The boss came to me and asked me if I'd like to go in as cookee. To which I said yes. I thought I'd like it.

I went in and the cook took a liking to me and I started in cooking. He showed me how to cook beans and bread and pies and biscuits. Soon I had two cookees under me. Two fellas that helped me. But I was the head cookee. That's how I learned to cook.

We had to feed the men good to keep em. You see, there was a gang that traveled. What we called them was camp inspectors. They'd come and stay two or three days and get filled up and go to another camp. They'd think it was better at the other camp, see.

Yes, they were big eaters! I've seen em take a plateful of beans and dump a whole cup full of sugar on top of em and eat em. That's the way they liked em—sweet.

That was the main thing in the morning. We had doughnuts. Biscuits. Eggs and bacon, sometimes. And ham.

At noon we had a regular dinner. We'd give em pie and potatoes and meat. The meat was frozen butts that had no bone in em at all. We'd cook them and they'd slice right off.

We didn't have any real butter; at that time margarine was white. They hadn't made it like they do now. That's all the camp had; the owner was trying to save money.

We had all tin dishes. Tin plates. The fork was a little, narrow, three-tine fork of iron. When we'd wash the spoons and knives and forks, we'd pour boiling water on em. Then we'd put em in a bran sack. One would get hold of one end and one the other and we'd dry em. Then we'd turn em back onto the table. We had to set the table twice for all those men. So we had to *work*!

At suppertime we'd give em meat and potatoes. 'Cause they're hearty eaters. They would eat as much in one meal as you'd eat in a day probably. They worked hard; that's why they ate so much.

At night we'd give em cake and pie and stuff like that. They could eat all they wanted.

Nobody talked at the table. We rang a bell and they'd all come in to eat. If they wanted something, they'd ask for it. But they never spoke. No, not a one. If they did, we put em out. When they finished their meal, they walked out and said nothing.

We had to clean up, that's why. When people go into a restaurant to eat, they set there and talk two or three hours and the waitress is waiting. We had to get them out to wash their dishes and to get the meals for the next men.

But we fed em good. They had all that they wanted to eat.

Almost all of the cooks I had were woods cooks. A woods cook starts in as I did right in the woods as a cookee; that's where he learns it. A woods cook ain't a cook that makes pastry like a hotel cook. They're two different cooks. The food is all put up different.

A hotel cook is no good in the woods. I had one one winter and he could cook bread and nice pastry, but he didn't know how to cook other stuff. He didn't know how to cook meat and potatoes. He got so ahead on meat that he put it in those bake tins; when he went out of the woods, I'll bet I threw out ten or fifteen big bake tins full of that meat. He didn't know how to cook a bushel of beans at a time like we did. A wood cook is no good in a hotel and a hotel cook is no good in the woods.

There were a lot of Polish fellas in that gang there. We called em Polacks, but they were Polish people. Some of em come right from Poland. They couldn't talk a word of English. They could do the work like cutting logs, but you had to go in the woods and show em or put em with another man and he'd tell em what to do.

Oh, the French, they could eat! The French was quite a feeder. Yessir! They could eat. They're rugged men. The year I worked up there in Victory, they locked a lot of fellas out of Canada. They had their homemade pants and woolen underwear.

The fella who taught me how to cook was a wonderful cook. Noel Bouchard, standing beside me there in the picture. He could cook! He was a brilliant fella and easy to get along with. Very, very calm. A nice disposition. After he left the camp, he went down in Massachusetts and learned the barber trade. He was smart in all of his work.

He showed me how to cook bread. He cooked wonderful bread. Great big loaves. We had great big pans. Christ, they'd hold a bushel or more. We made the dough and put it in that and let it rise. It had yeast in it and flour and all the ingredients. That bread would rise. We'd break it down and let it come up again. The next time

Jim King (far right)

we'd take and work it on the bread board. And cut it the way we
wanted to put it in the pans. And let it rise. When it rose up a certain
amount, we'd stick it in the oven for thirty-five and forty minutes.
We'd make some thirty, forty, or fifty loaves.

I used to cook a bushel or more of beans a day.

I could cook doughnuts. Hell, I cooked doughnuts one day
when I was teaching this boy how to cook, see. There was something I forgot to put in. And I fried the doughnuts. I had about six
men working for me that spring. It was just springing out then. We
couldn't break camp and we had all the horses to take care of. So
we logged and it was muddy. I fried the doughnuts and I went up
to work the roads. When I came down, the boy had the doughnuts
all hung on nails around the door. They were so hard that you
could drive em right through that board. Something I didn't put
in.

The men would each eat a half-dozen doughnuts. And two,
three, five, six biscuits, too.

I had a Polish fella up in the camp and my cook sliced a whole
big plate of nice roast pork. By God, that man cleaned off the
whole business. The plate was heaped right up and he took it all
and ate it. Probably two or three pounds of pork.

Madeleine Kunin

GOVERNOR OF VERMONT

Montpelier, Vermont
Born: 1933

➤➤➤➤➤➤➤➤➤➤➤➤➤➤➤ ⊛ ◄◄◄◄◄◄◄◄◄◄◄◄◄◄◄◄◄

MADELEINE MAY KUNIN MADE HISTORY in January 1985 by taking office as Vermont's first woman governor, by being only the third Democratic governor, and by accomplishing all this despite not being a native Vermonter. State tradition holds that three generations are necessary to make someone a Vermonter. Even so, a candidate for native Vermonter still might not pass muster without also being a rock-ribbed Republican.

Kunin was born to a Jewish family in Zurich, Switzerland in 1933. She escaped the Holocaust to America in 1940; five of her relatives were not so lucky and were killed by the Nazis. Although trained as a journalist during the 1950s, Madeleine Kunin spent most of her adult life as a housewife. In the early 1970s, a return visit to Switzerland activated a political spark in her. Later she said that her escape on the last American ship out of Italy had been an early, if at the time unappreciated, politicizing experience.

I think that the Kunin story can best be understood as the American norm rather than the exception. As she has said of the early years she spent in America with her mother and brother, "the whole Horatio Alger myth was alive and well as far as we were concerned. I think everyone who comes here, who has the immigrant experience, carries with them a certain set of values for life." Governor Kunin denies having had a single political mentor, but in her inaugural address she did dwell on sources of strength she found in her family's women, especially in her mother. Mrs. May did not live long enough to see her daughter take the oath of office in Montpelier, but every Vermonter knows of her courage in pulling herself away from home to board that last ship escaping Genoa, Italy.

> I stand with the memory of members of my family who are no longer with me—my mother, my aunt, my grandmother—the strong women who could never have dreamt I would be in this

place on this day, but who, through the courage of their own lives, give me the stamina to stand as tall as they did in their time.

It was my mother, who as a widow, came to America from Switzerland with two small children, aged six and ten, in 1940, as war was spreading over Europe.

In addition to a limited knowledge of English, she carried with her to these shores a limitless dream of what this country could offer her and her children.

And she talked to us about the dream. It was not until many years later that I fully understood her.

Her dream enabled me to strive, to reach, and to touch some horizons I was certain were beyond my grasp.

Madeleine Kunin

Eleanor Roosevelt and Adlai Stevenson were probably two of the people who were influential in shaping my thinking. Eleanor Roosevelt because she was a woman and because she was unusual and because she was very humanitarian. My mother admired her. She was kind of the woman of the times. People would read her column every day. She was highly regarded.

Stevenson for his wit and his language. He seemed to symbolize the things I believed in.

But in both of those cases I never thought of myself entering into politics. They were just people I admired.

On the Vermont scene, Phil Hoff was as much of a role model as anybody when I first got interested in politics. Because of the kinds of issues he addressed. His energy. His youth. And the fact that he was willing to change things.

But I didn't ask him for advice the first time I ran. There was no single mentor or person I can look back at who changed my life. My life didn't work that way. It was many things. Everybody's life is made up of a mosaic of people and events.

For instance, when I was in Switzerland in 1970, they were having a referendum on women having the vote in national elections. They already had the vote in their cantons, which are similar to our states. The Women's Movement was starting here. The fact that women were being elected to the Zurich city council and that there was a woman mayor of Geneva — even though women didn't have the vote in federal elections — struck me as very ironic. In the United States I knew very few women who held office. I thought that that's what I would be interested in when I came back to the United States.

Sometimes you see your country better from afar than when you're in the middle of it.

Ludolphe "Doc" La Bounty

ICE FISHERMAN

Barton, Vermont
Born: 1907

➤➤➤➤➤➤➤➤➤➤➤➤➤➤➤➤➤ ✵ ◄◄◄◄◄◄◄◄◄◄◄◄◄◄◄◄◄◄

FISH SHANTY FISHING FOR TROUT is a relatively new institution in Vermont and Doc La Bounty of Barton opposes it. Yet as often as possible he jigs for trout in his wood-heated fish house and tends his tip-ups outside on the twenty-four-inch ice of Crystal Lake.

When Doc La Bounty was a boy, ice fishing for trout was illegal but winter fishing for cusk, pickerel, and perch was all right. In fact, his best memories are of chiseling holes in the ice with sharpened automobile springs and standing outside in the elements all day with his uncles fishing for pickerel.

Doc says that the last decades of winter trout fishing have put too much pressure on the fish and that they can neither multiply adequately nor grow into the hefty specimens he dreams about. But who can say? Hunting and fishing regulations excite as much passion among sportsmen as the size of remembered buck or trout. All I knew last January was that after passing so many Vermont lakes dotted with fishing shanties I was very curious to meet an ice fisherman.

Doc is the nickname Ludolphe La Bounty acquired through playing a doctor in a grammar school play in Barton. A lucky acquisition, the nickname differentiated Ludolphe from his nearest siblings, Rodolphe and Adolphe.

What a family of brothers and uncles it must have been. Doc's father had two brothers and Doc himself seven. The La Bountys were a fun-loving crew. I was lucky enough to experience some of their old-style conviviality when I visited Doc one winter evening. His large, modern house resounded with a constant hubbub of visitors. The talk was a heady bouillabaisse of ice fishing: favorite spots, methods, great catches of the past, and who was catching what now. The gossip of the ice.

Among the merrymakers was Doc's nephew, Luce, his present fishing buddy now that the last of his favorite uncles has died. Those uncles, Aimé and Simeon, are the subject of much of this chapter. Obviously Doc was very close to them. "We used to have a lot of fun," he says wistfully. "Always telling stories and talking about fishing."

And, no doubt, about stone cutting, since these La Bountys all worked in Vermont's famous granite sheds. (In 1940 the Federal Writers Project spent a year in Barre collecting more than one hundred interviews with granite workers. Some of those interviews are available in Ann Banks's *First-Person America*.) The significance of granite cutting for the present story is that when Doc's Uncle Aimé died young of stonecutter's tuberculosis, Doc left the sheds forever; in fact, he is living into a ripe old age as the dean of local ice fishermen.

Fish, not stone, is my subject here. Doc and I went down the lake that night to help one of his brothers, whose four-wheel drive vehicle had gotten stuck at the landing. In that dim light, we worked our shovels to free the truck's wheels and bumper. Offshore, the faint, square shapes of fish houses beckoned from the plain of ice.

I was back early the next morning. (Early for me, anyway, but very late by ice fishermen's standards.) I have to admit that the novelty of being out on the ice, even in Doc's big truck, was reason for a bit of unease. The newspapers had been full of the disappearance of a distance-skating doctor on Lake Memphremagog. Doc assured me that he never went out on thin ice, though many other people took foolish chances.

Like the vast majority of Vermont's ice shanties, Doc's was home-built. His veteran plywood box was about twenty-five years old. "There are better-looking fish houses," he said, "but we got a lot of fish out of this one." The shack was forty-six inches wide (to fit a pick-up truck) and eight feet long, though ten feet is the common length, to make loading and unloading easier. Plywood outside and cardboard inside, the shack had a jerry-built wood stove and a look of having seen some rough winters. Fish hooks hung from the cardboard walls and from random nails. Tackle and bait were ready for action, as were coffee cups and a deck of cards. On one wall I noticed a penciled list that detailed Doc's hours fishing, and his meager catch, this season.

Doc and Luce take their trout fishing very seriously, but nothing they did that day worked. They sat beside the greenish ice hole bobbing jig sticks up and down. "If you bring somebody out here," Doc said, "you hardly ever get a bite." Fishing is full of rules like that and fish, bless their little hearts, always play by the rules.

After about an hour of talk and jigging, Doc jumped up. "Hey, you want some lunch? I got hot dogs and cookies for you." He went to work stoking up the old barrel stove and frying hot dogs. I couldn't believe how warm the little room was getting. Smoke poured from the antique stove, which Doc described as "more natural" than the new gas rigs. Finally he laughed, "This is a cook-out because we have to open the door to let the smoke out."

We heard a skidoo snarling across the ice toward us. Doc looked out and said that his friend, the game warden, was checking licenses and catches in each fish house. "He's probably saying he doesn't have to check here because La Bounty don't catch any fish anyway."

Naturally the big, green-suited man's visit produced more hearty talk. I was surprised to learn about locally notorious poachers and their attacks on game wardens. Of course, we also heard how many of the neighboring fish houses were eating trout rather than hot dogs.

Doc motioned toward a nearby blue shack. "Them guys," he said, "got here at six o'clock this morning and they got ten, twelve, fifteen lines out there. It stands to reason they'd get more fish."

Fortified by lunch, the La Bountys went back to serious fishing. But the luck of the ice was against them. "Those damn fish don't bite very good," said Doc.

"Amen," said the fish.

I ain't got nothing to be very proud of the last three or four years. About seven years ago, I got fifty trout. About half legal. I got two or three pretty good ones that year. One eight pound and another about four pound.

There are nowhere near as many fish now as when I was a boy. And most of the fish we catch today are stocked fish. If they didn't stock these lakes, we probably wouldn't catch anything. Oh, once in awhile we catch a native fish; you can tell cause they're more stocky and have nicer color to em. Nice white fins.

There were definitely more trout fifty years ago. Of course, we couldn't ice fish for em then. There was a law against it. Oh, I'm against this fishing myself, see. I don't like it. But everybody else is doing it so I might as well join em. But they get too many trout. They fish all night and all day and the fish don't have any chance to grow or multiply.

Ice fishing is a big event. I like to come out here and meet people. But as far as catching the fish, that ain't the biggest point. Like those guys over there, they want me to come look at their fish later. Oh, there's beer and whiskey. A lot of people bring lunch.

Some people will spit in the hole. And throw cigarette butts and cigars. Then the cigars will dissolve and . . . I don't allow anybody to throw butts in my hole. I don't think much of em myself. They should know better. I tell em that when they fish in *my* fish house I can't have that.

"Doc" LaBounty

One fella told me to put kerosene in the hole so it wouldn't freeze over. [*Laughter.*] You pull a fish out of a kerosene hole and the fish wouldn't be no good. [*Laughter.*] Oh boy, you see everything.

Me and my Uncle Simeon were up at Willoughby Lake one time fishing for trout and we'd had a few beers. There were some other guys out there fishing who were pretty well under the weather. "Well," one of em says, "let's have another bottle of beer and see if we can get a bite or not." Poor Uncle Simeon, he never forgot that. Every once in awhile he'd say, "Hey Doc, let's have another bottle of beer. Maybe we'll catch a fish."

The best fun my Uncle Simeon and I had was ice fishing up at Newport. We used to get a lot of nice pickerel. Of course, in them days you could catch twenty-five pounds of pickerel. We'd get a little bit over twenty five sometimes on a good day.

At the beginning of the season, the first thing you do is move your fish house out. I take it out the week before fishing. Set it up and get it ready. If the ice ain't thick enough to drive on, we have to walk out. We make some holes with the motor auger. You got the right to fish with eight lines. Eight tip-ups. A tip-up is a device where when the fish bites the bait the flag goes up, then you know you've got a bite.

Sometimes out on the ice you can't see very good. It's foggy. All white. And them fish houses, the snow always drifts around em.

When me and Uncle Simeon used to go up to Newport to fish for pickerel, we walked out on the ice 'cause we didn't have no four-wheel drive vehicles like we have today. We'd go up there with hand chisels and cut ten holes apiece through two-foot-thick ice and fish all day and think nothing of it. But them days, it was different than it is today.

The chisel was about five feet long. We made them out of automobile springs. We'd take a spring from a car and cut it down to about fourteen inches long, then grind it down on an emery, and make a handle for it.

Uncle Aimé and I cut stone together for years before he died of that granite disease. Granite TB from cutting granite. I worked in that for eighteen years cutting grave monuments and vaults. I used to cut the roof parts and a couple of other guys would cut the sides. Most of our work was monuments. When my Uncle Aimé died, I was working with him and it scairt me. 'Cause he was sick about a year and half. When he died, it really made me think. I never went back. I guess I was lucky.

I born in 1907 and I started to fish when I was twelve. My uncle came along and said, "C'mon Ludolphe." He didn't call me Doc 'cause I didn't have my name then. So we went down to the head of the lake here and we anchored and we fished about an hour and a half. No bites. So Uncle Aimé says, "Let's move. We'll pick em up and go somewhere else." I didn't have much of a rig to fish with; he'd let me use a pole he had. So I started reeling my line in. I said, "I'm caught on a snag, Uncle Aimé. I'm caught."

"Let me see it," he said. So I handed him the pole. "Heck," he said, "you got a fish on there." And he reeled it in. It weighed nine pounds.

Boy, after that I used to like to go trout fishing. [*Laughter.*] So I started then with my father and my Uncle Aimé La Bounty and we done a lot of trout fishing. Uncle Aimé was a great fisherman. He got some nice fish out of this lake.

In winter he used to fish outdoors, not in ice houses, at Parker Pond. It was cold fishing outside. I remember one time he and another guy were going up. I was just a kid, thirteen, and I was supposed to go with em, but it was pretty cold. So Uncle Aimé told his friend, "We probably hadn't better take Ludolphe."

My mother told me in the morning that it was so cold that Uncle Aimé had decided not to take me. I said, "By gosh, I'm going anyway."

My mother said, "Oh no, you hadn't better walk up there by yourself."

But I walked up and found em on the ice fishing. So my Uncle Aimé said, "You want to fish?"

I said, "Yeah."

He said, "I'll put you out a couple of lines."

We fished a couple of hours and my flag went up. I went over and pulled it in and I had a five-pound cusk. Boy, that was really something. [*Laughter.*] That was quite a fish for me. I never forgot it.

My Uncle Aimé was a little bit better off than my father was. My father had twelve kids. He just worked around at odd jobs. He had one fish pole and one line but my Uncle Aimé, he had two because he was making more money and he could afford it. That's how come in summer me and my brother fished with him. He let me take a pole first because I was oldest. Then after I got my fish, it was my brother's turn to fish.

You probably won't believe it, but one night my brother Rodolphe and myself and my dad and my Uncle Aimé went out and anchored our boat in the lake here and fished for trout. Uncle Aimé says, "You fish first, Ludolphe, and then you get one and let Rodolphe in."

OK, we went to fishing. In a little while I got one. Seven pounds.

Then Rudi, he took over the pole. And he got a seven pounder.

We each got a fish that night and they all weighed over seven pounds. You ought to have seen them fish! Some like that! Unbelievable. You can't catch fish like that out here now. That was sixty-five years ago.

My Uncle Simeon died here four or five years ago. He and I done a lot of ice fishing. We had a little jigging stick for trout and then we had these tip-ups, too. Oh, we'd visit and eat. You know how a guy'll do. There's always somebody comes by.

I don't play cards much anymore because my eyes bother me. But when I was young, I always had my cards in my pocket. When I'd see my Uncle Simeon, I'd say, "C'mon Uncle Simeon, let's have a game of cards" and we'd play. Oh boy, years ago! He was a good card player and he taught me to play cribbage. We usually played cribbage and pitch. Pitch is high-low jack.

Uncle Simeon was a little bit older than me. We were together for years in the granite sheds at Hardwick, Barre, a lot of other places. He was a polisher and I was a cutter. We drove back and forth all summer to Hardwick.

Oh, he was a nice guy. He was one of the best uncles I had. Him and my Uncle Aimé. They were more my line—hunting and fishing.

Carl Lawrence

DAIRYMAN

St. Johnsbury, Vermont
Born: 1904

➤➤➤➤➤➤➤➤➤➤➤➤➤➤➤ ✳ ◄◄◄◄◄◄◄◄◄◄◄◄◄◄◄◄◄◄◄

CARL LAWRENCE PEDDLED MILK from the time he was "big enough to carry a milk bottle." As a boy, he helped his grandfather sell milk retail in St. Johnsbury, which was near their Crow Hill farm. Carl's grandfather was a St. Johnsbury selectman and road commissioner, a no-nonsense fellow who "if he had something to say, he'd say it so that you could hear it all right." Every morning before breakfast the two of them and their Morgan horse visited each customer's front door or porch. In winter their milk wagon was remounted on sled runners for the snowy, daily trip.

Wasn't that slave labor? "No," Carl says. "Everything was better then—the relationship between the kids and all the people. I think that we had better times than today's kids."

The Lawrences—Carl, his older brother, his father, and grandfather—and three or four hired men produced and sold the milk from about twenty cows. Without middle men, this was the heyday of dairy profitability. Pasteurization and other costly processes never came between the teat and the town. And labor was very cheap.

Labor, however, was the Achilles heel of the operation. The Lawrence milk-peddling operation ceased during World War I, when the hired hands abandoned the farm for excitement overseas. The milk wagon was sold and the Lawrence milk bottles gradually disappeared from circulation.

To understand why Carl Lawrence spent a lifetime on the farm, consider the place's comfortable associations. Every corner of the Crow Hill farm echoes strongly with Lawrence family history. Some of its giant maple trees were planted by his great-grandfather, whom he vaguely remembers. (That worthy founded Vermont's first grange, Green Mountain No. 1, just after the Civil War.)

Carl's explanation of why he stuck with farming emphasizes "the way of living"—working with horses, growing things. He remembers a time when everybody trusted everybody and when people were always ready to help their neighbors.

Some people are as attuned to farm life as wild animals are to the seasons. Carl Lawrence's brothers were not born farmers; they left for other jobs as soon as possible. "They decided that there was an easier way to make a living than farming," Carl says. "I was just dumb enough to stay. I liked the way of living, I guess. That's as near as I can get to it."

The following vignette about the difference between Carl and his older brother is full of unexpressed love for hay, horses, weather, and hills. "My older brother and I were about the same age. We worked together for years when we were growing up. I always drove the team because he didn't want to have anything to do with that. Of course, when we'd come in after haying or anything I'd have to put the team in and feed them before I'd go to dinner. He'd jump off and go into the house and wash up and be ready to eat. He didn't want to bother with putting the team in.

"But that little extra time never bothered me. It didn't seem like that much work to me. It was just part of the day."

I used to go with my grandfather for a number of years peddling milk. We used to get along together pretty well. He was a selectman, road commissioner, and quite a lot of things in St. Johnsbury.

I always respected him. Any decision he made was most always right. I just had a feeling he was right. When he said something had to be done, it had to be done. That's all. Like the wood box in the kitchen had to be filled up twice a day from wood in the woodshed.

We peddled door to door in town for years. There isn't any of that anymore. When I was twelve, fourteen years old there were about thirty or thirty-five farmers who peddled milk in the town of St. Johnsbury. Now there isn't one.

Each farmer had his own customers he delivered to every day. Quite a lot of farmers had bottles with their own names on em. [*Laughter.*] But they were soon mixed up; everybody had everybody's.

We didn't go like they do today. We used to keep it this side of Railroad Street. We never used to go over in the east side of town; that was too far. I don't think our round trip would be more than five miles, unless you got in some extry trips to pick up something.

We carried bottles of milk. Or cans. A lot of it was in cans, them

Carl Lawrence

days. There were different sizes — ten quart, eight quart — which we used mostly when we peddled local. When we went to the creamery, we took bigger ones.

We had a kind of a covered wagon with a canvas top. It had a seat and a walkway in the middle. It was open in front. Where you walked in, there was a box about 2½ feet high with a cover on it. You put your bottles in there. There was another narrower one under the seat. We used to put the bottles of cream and the small pints of milk in there. Then in the back there was a bigger box where we used to put cans and what extra bottles we had.

We had that wagon made special by John Ryan in a wagon shop where Railroad Street and Portland Street go together. There's a filling station there now.

The trick to selling milk was to have it fresh. We'd start about six o'clock in the morning to deliver and we'd get to most places in time so they'd have it for breakfast. Most people in those days didn't have refrigerators. They'd either set it down on the cellar floor or out on the back step to keep it cold.

We used to deliver the milk in a ten-quart can and pour it out with a measure. They'd have a container of their own. Either a bowl or some kind of a dish. They'd set it on the step between the doors or in the hallway. Or just inside an outside door. And lots of times out on the porch. Then the cats and the dogs would come along, knock the cover off, and have a little drink. Not too sanitary! It wouldn't pass nowadays, but I don't think anybody died from it.

We delivered *every* day in those days. Your life depended on it. Seven days a week. Why, the world would come to an end if you missed a day.

My grandfather used to get up around three o'clock and go out and feed the cows their hay when they were milking a lot. The hired man would get up around four and start milking. After grandfather had fed the cows, he would bottle up the milk. Then he'd be in the house getting ready to go to town to deliver it about six o'clock in the morning.

Later on it used to be my job to feed and clean the horses. I had to feed em hay first thing in the morning cause it would take em half to three-quarters of an hour to eat up the hay. Then I brushed em off before we got ready to go. We just used one horse delivering. Morgans were the toughest and could stand it the best.

When the war came along, the farm help'd go and work in Fairbanks's a month or so. A farm worker who joined the service directly got a lot less pay than a factory worker because a factory worker was considered skilled. Then they'd go join the Army and get bigger pay.

We gave the milk route up before the war ended. Probably in 1917 or 1918.

I liked to work with the horses when we used to work with em all the time. Twas a good way to farm. I think it still would be. The only problem with it would be the expense of the manpower. You've got to pay a man so much now that it would ruin you financially. A tractor with one man to operate it will do the work of four or five teams. You'd need five or six men to do that work with teams. The price of them men would put you on the town farm.

Maude Lund

TOWN CLERK

Granby, Vermont
Born: 1911

➤➤➤➤➤➤➤➤➤➤➤➤➤➤➤ ⊗ ◄◄◄◄◄◄◄◄◄◄◄◄◄◄◄◄◄

THE BEST THING ABOUT VERMONT TOWN governance is that it allows ordinary people to do extraordinary things. Consider Maude Lund, long-time town clerk and treasurer of Granby, Vermont (population, 82). As her story here makes clear, she grew up at a time of limited opportunities by 1980s Vermont standards. I was amazed, for instance, that at the time of her election to the state legislature she had never been to Montpelier, not so very far away from her Northeast Kingdom home. (Granby is so isolated that when people leave town they are said to be "going out.") The journey she has made, however, far exceeds measurement in miles.

Granby is a faded lumber town where most of the fifty-three voters are related to each other. It *is* small. But federal and state regulations apply as much to it as to the largest center. In Granby, Maude Lund is the elected official who keeps the business of government businesslike for the voters and for the town selectmen and school directors.

Not long ago Granby and Victory residents faced and solved a crisis that could easily have daunted less self-sufficient souls. Residents wanted electricity; the power company said "No." What? "*Electricity?*" you say. "Were those people living in the Dark Ages?" No, not at all. They were simply still living like Vermonters always had. They didn't finally enter the age of appliances, televisions, and garage door-openers until 1963.

But Maude Lund's story is not really about technology. In bringing electricity to their town, Maude Lund and her neighbors in Granby and Victory had done the impossible. An accomplishment like that makes me want to stand up and cheer. Especially since I know about the little girl who couldn't go to her one-room school in winter because of the long distance. I know about the teacher who in six formative years created a life-long passion for civic affairs in a small child. And the young person who overcame her educational disappointments to go on to help where help was needed most.

I don't want to make this sound like a Fourth of July speech. Nor do I want to claim that Maude Lund symbolizes this or that. Actually she is a very folksy person who sincerely likes to participate in her town, school, family, and circle of friends. She and we are fortunate to have lived in places where such participation is unfettered.

And because Granby is fortunate, too, it dedicated its 1985 Town Report to Maude Lund in honor of her twenty-five years of service as town clerk and treasurer.

I owe a lot to my parents because they were hardworking people and they brought up a large family. My father was a certified public accountant. My mother was just as smart as he was, but she didn't have the education.

I went to the one-room school at Walden Four Corners. We walked more than three miles to school. I just went in the fall and spring in my first years. In winter my mother taught me at home. It was a little too far for a small girl to walk in winter.

We used to snowshoe down off the mountain in winter because my father would run out of chewing tobacco. He was a very hard-working man. A college grad but he still preferred the woods and flowers and working up to Caspian Lake, and cutting cordwood, and trapping. But he would run out of tobacco. American Navy or Yankee Girl. And when he ever ran out, boy, you'd better get your snowshoes on and hike to the Bend. It wasn't anything for us kids to go down cross-country for coffee and a gallon of kerosene and, "get that tobacco." Mother got so she would hide some, so in an emergency she'd have it for Dad so he wouldn't send anybody or go out himself in a bad storm. You see, Dad *had* to have the tobacco. He went regardless of the weather. Or we did.

I had a happy childhood and happy school days. In fact, when I left school, the last two days, I couldn't eat my lunch with the schoolchildren because I felt so bad about leaving them.

Of course, it's a wonder we didn't die with germs. There was no such thing as any storm windows at school. Just single panes of glass. And a big wood stove. When we got there, the janitor had the fire going. If it was really cold, Mrs. Sweatt would play the piano and get us to exercising.

We had to bring our own water cups, soap, and hand towels. We furnished our own hot lunches. But we raised money for a

Conservo-Canner that we put our little jars of food in and got them hot on top of the wood stove. Then we took our own dishes home and washed them.

We had eight grades and about thirty scholars.

When I was in first grade, a new teacher, Mae E. Sweatt, took over the school after a period of indiscipline. She was an experienced teacher and mother and her discipline. . . She just took right over and you felt it the minute she stood up there.

She was good to us. She watched every move we made. I got along fine. I did two grades in one year.

Everybody liked her. She taught from the minute she entered school. She taught on the school grounds. We didn't have anything like they do nowadays. We took our own balls and bats to school. We made up our own games. While we were walking to school, we picked flowers and she gave prizes. We had parties to raise money for things for school.

She could play the piano. She taught us patriotism and respect of the flag. We picked flowers and made wreaths for the soldiers' graves. There was lots of singing and lots of fun and lots of studying, nine to four.

She kept us busy. The minute you got any work done and you sat there her eyes were on you and she had something ready for you. In sixth grade she asked me to balance her attendance record book. I felt quite honored.

Mrs. Sweatt was real rabid about teaching us to write and spell and do arithmetic. She really drilled us. Mrs. Sweatt was the type of person . . . I mean she taught you to march. She took pains with our personal appearance. She cared about our health. She watched our manners during recess and noon. She praised us if we did well; but if we didn't, we got reprimanded.

Like poetry. That's something that is a big comfort to me. When I'm alone I'll grab a Vermont historical reader with those nice Vermont poems in it. She didn't just say take your seat and study a poem. She took every line and picked it right apart and made us tell what we saw in that one line. She taught!

And she visited every parent during the school year. Right after school she went to the homes with her horse and buggy. She would ask when it would be convenient for her to call. Naturally I loved that because my mother would get out the doilies and put ferns on a pretty stand and we would have a nice harvest supper.

She met every parent and she knew what kind of a home those children came from. And she tried to help us.

In those days eighth grade farm boys were pretty big boys. They were men grown, many of those boys. But not one of them was ever mean to me. I was on their ball team. Although I was little, I had walked to school so much and had been with brothers so much that we played a lot of games together. Mrs. Sweatt taught gymnastics. She put a ladder up across out in the shed for the boys to chin the bar. I tell you, she kept you busy!

In the winter, on Vermont Day, Mrs. Sweatt would devote the rest of the afternoon to just Vermont. We'd read poems about Vermont and make maps. It was fun. I remembered those things when I saw the inscriptions on the State House. I had never visited Montpelier until I became a representative.

I had Mrs. Sweatt from first to sixth grade. Because the smaller children got out in the afternoon early, it just left a handful of us there. She wanted to keep us pretty busy, so she thought we should form a literary club. I was the secretary and my brother George was the president. We got interested in picking up current events. Of course, I liked civil government. That's probably where it started. I enjoyed my civil government. And then we started to go to town meeting. Well, I was fascinated.

I got out of school at fourteen. I couldn't go on to high school because we lived way up on Walden Mountain. It was a large family. I wanted to go to St. Johnsbury Academy, but my dad didn't feel like sending his little daughter away there to school.

Two of my former teachers came to help me at home with high school subjects. So I read and studied and I got our and worked in the surrounding towns: Greensboro, North Greensboro, Walden Mountain, Danville, and North Walden.

I used to go help my married brother. We went to town meeting together. My parents hadn't taken the time to go off Walden Mountain to town meeting. But when I began to get out, I saw what fun town meeting was. I love to have a few arguments!

Town meeting lasted all day over in Walden. I'm telling you, they tore everything apart. Roads weren't even plowed in those days; I was there when they began to talk about plowing them. Those farmers, they didn't want any plowed roads. They had their horses and double sleds taking the milk to Greensboro Bend.

I loved to see those old farmers get up there and fight. I really was with the farmers. I didn't want to see everything upset.

I was married when I was eighteen and I came to Granby. Well, the man I married was a selectman here. He worked on the roads and he was right up and acoming in the town business. He loved it. He was chairman of the board.

Of course, I always like to read and write, so when he was gone

I would help out by reading his papers and doing things for him. I became a school director and I was a library trustee and an auditor and a trustee of my church.

He was twenty five then, but he only lived seven years before he died of a congenital heart condition. We had three small children.

After he died, my brother-in-law was a selectman and a road commissioner. So there again I was right in town work. Then I married my brother-in-law in 1948. I kept books for him. In 1952 our town clerk/treasurer was taken sick and I was elected.

I've always taken a keen interest in everything. I was in the legislature in 1963 and 1964 as a representative on the Government Operations Committee, just like a town, only bigger.

Sometimes town work is enough to drive you crazy. Reports to the federal government and the state of Vermont. See, we don't have a copier or a computer. It is a small town but the same laws apply, so you always have to make reports.

I worked for twelve years with no salary. I had my commission, which used to be a couple of hundred dollars and maybe $300 in fees. That was what I had for about twelve years. Then after I had my house wired for electricity in 1963, I bought a few secondhand appliances. Well, I just couldn't pay my bills anymore. So I went out to St. Johnsbury to work. When I came back, the town eventually gave me $100 a month. That and my fees and my tax commission.

Town meeting is a great experience. I have attended almost every one in my adult life. Once in awhile I missed when I was working out.

Town meeting is a wonderful chance for people to govern themselves. And I get right after them here; I get the young folks registered and get them out. Probably 80 percent come. Sometimes we've had 100 percent. In a small town where it affects them directly, their interest is high. They have children in school and they do their own road work. When we had reappraisal, our own listers did it.

I take a lot of responsibility before the town meeting. For instance, I find out who is going out of office and who is running. The selectmen don't make a budget, which they are supposed to do, but I talk with them and I know about the money. I do a lot to keep things running smoothly. The selectmen are good at the physical labor. They and I meet often. I do the same with the school board.

There's a lot of work to having a town meeting. A lot of laws to be followed. Getting out the checklists. Meeting deadlines. Getting out the warning. The warning is a list of articles to be voted

Maude Lund

on. You can't raise money unless it's in there by a specific article. Raising money for the schools and for the town. Electing officers.

Each town has its own individual warning. The selectmen are in charge of the warning. There are some statewide issues, but we steer clear of anything that's pretty big that we don't know much about. This year we are including one about whether we should have a bicentennial license plate on the front of cars. They only want to know if we are in favor of it; it isn't binding.

The town clerk keeps all of the minutes and is clerk at the elections. It's a long day.

We have had some very interesting town meetings. There's always keen interest. I think the people are always pretty well organized before they attend. They know who they want to vote for. We have a unique situation in Granby because we have fifty-three voters and thirty five of them are related as family or as in-laws. The young marrieds are parents of children in school.

We have town meeting in the evening now. We used to always have it in the daytime. It was a long affair where we had the school in and we had dinner and all that. But now the men work in the woods and they want it in the evening. But we are very well organized when we go there, so the town meeting moves right through. We have a good moderator, a retired man who has donated a lot of time to the town. And while we all have a chance to speak, we don't have much chance to argue. He keeps order real well.

Until 1963 it was kerosene lamps in Granby. Washing on the board. Ironing with a wood stove. Our refrigeration was ice cold spring water.

In the late fifties, a few people got together with the county agent and we began to talk about getting electricity. We notified Central Vermont, but they really didn't want to come in here because we had so few houses and because the power would have to come from Lancaster, New Hampshire. They quoted us a huge price we never could have paid.

But we didn't give up. We organized. And we publicized our plight. We told the executive secretary of Northeastern Vermont Development that we didn't have any resources. He said, "Of course, you *do*. You're a lumbering town that's died. Why don't you use your lumbering background to have a foliage holiday in the fall and put on a meal?" Well, we didn't have any place to put one on. And he said, "Why not build a lumber camp?" We didn't have any money, but the men said they would build a lumber camp if the women would cook the dinner.

That's what we did. We called it Holiday in the Hills and we had a lot of company.

And that began to get our plight out around. We still didn't get very far, but we kept ahaving Holiday in the Hills. It grew very popular; it turned into a two day affair and thousands of people came. The reporters from Massachusetts and New York picked it up and spread it across the country.

We knew we were entitled to electricity. So we just kept working and we embarrassed the power company. Our congressman and our senators visited us at the Cook Shack.

We got our power in 1963 at a reasonable price. And we still have Holiday in the Hills.

I think I enjoy my lights the best of everything because I *do* like to read.

People said when I first left Walden Mountain for Granby, "Going way up to Granby?" When I got to Granby, there was lots of social life at the Town Hall. We had lots of dances and parties and picnics and fishing in the Connecticut River. We really had a lot of good times here.

I don't know whether electricity changed it or not, but our younger people now go out to social things because they all have their cars. Better income. Better education. We have the little school things, but we don't have town meeting dinners and we don't gather at the church with a Christmas tree like we used to do. But I think most of the people in town are happy with their own arrangement because so many of em are related. They have a big Thanksgiving and Christmas.

Oh, I like modern things, but when I was younger with three children, I and the other parents around here could really swing this work pretty good. I used to work out in the hay field and raise a garden and potatoes. We had cows and pigs and hens.

Young people today have more opportunities, but they don't take care of themselves as well as they could. I don't believe I saw three overweight children when I was a girl. Because girls helped with the washing and the housework and they walked to school. Boys brought in wood and helped with the chores. Now diets are all you hear about.

I have often thought of Mrs. Sweatt. I don't even know where she's buried. But if I did, I would visit her grave. It seems as though everything I learned in school I learned from Mrs. Sweatt.

Brewster Martin, M.D.

COUNTRY DOCTOR

Chelsea, Vermont
Born: 1922

➤➤➤➤➤➤➤➤➤➤➤➤➤➤➤ ✳ ◄◄◄◄◄◄◄◄◄◄◄◄◄◄◄◄

COUNTRY DOCTORS SUPPOSEDLY RODE OFF into American history long ago and have not been heard from since. In Vermont, as elsewhere, those horse-and-buggy physicians delivered generations of babies, eased countless childhood traumas, and were often present at life's end. Modern medicine, transportation, and society have created a new doctor whose knowledge, wealth, and status far exceed anything imagined by any nineteenth-century sawbones. The old ways—the house calls and the personal attention—are obsolete.

In Vermont they are not impossible to find.

Dr. Brewster Martin of Chelsea still makes house calls back in the mountains, where so many of his patients live. He has the white hair and soothing, bedside manner that would make him a most welcome visitor to my sickroom. He is a thoughtful, caring man; in short, everything one could wish for in a doctor. He is a compassionate link between the old rural medical practice and modern "health care delivery systems."

Not only has medicine changed since he first opened for business in 1953 but the countryside has changed, too. His original rut-plagued automobile trips over the mountains to isolated farms near Vershire and Corinth are now—mostly—aided by paved roads. Whereas farming was then the area's predominant occupation, today Dr. Martin can only think of six or seven full-time farmers. In addition to new occupations, there has been a great influx of newcomers escaping urban realities.

But Dr. Martin says that the community's people have not changed any more than its physical appearance. "There was more land cleared then," he says, "but if you look at pictures of this little town of Chelsea taken a hundred years ago, other than the low income housing for seniors it really doesn't look that much different. The people haven't changed; they're just doing something different."

The essence of Dr. Martin's practice has remained remarkably constant. "I know families," he says, "I don't just know people." He is very proud of the fact that he is now taking care of children of parents who themselves he delivered. "I played the organ at a wedding recently of a child I delivered — and that's a thrill."

In our mobile society, Dr. Martin is a small part of the glue, the continuity, that holds things together. To me, his role looks very satisfying and enviable. "It's been a great life," he says with his elfin smile. "I can't imagine not wanting to go to the office in the morning."

Nevertheless, the burdens must sometimes seem overwhelming. I am thinking not just about the people who think they *must* call at six A.M. about their flu symptoms but also about those life or death situations where the doctor's best efforts cannot prevail and where someone, probably a friend, dies in front of his eyes.

How does he cope with such stress? Distancing is an important way — as when he reads a fading, penciled warning about smoking and lung cancer to a complaining patient. "I haul out the chart and say, 'Here's my note twenty years ago. It says, Stop smoking. You made the choice. Obviously you're a gambler. You gambled that you would be one of the 15 percent of the people who would not develop this from smoking and you lost. I'm very sorry for you, but it was your decision.'" For someone who loves people as much as Brewster Martin does, that speech must be very difficult to make.

The repetitiousness of the job must also be trying. For instance, the day before my visit he had seen thirty-two people in his office, including ten sore throat cases. He told me that long ago an old doctor reminded him that behind every sore throat there is a different human being: You have learn to get past the sore throat to the person so that "you're not looking at the same telephone pole every time."

For Dr. Martin, artistic expression is an extremely important part of life, whether singing in his church's choir, or playing the piano, or painting, or even making his own clothes. He directs a small theater company in Chelsea, is an inveterate letter-writer, a hardy parent, and an avid skier. Townspeople think he is indefatigable.

Humor is an essential part of his makeup. Never a day goes by that he and his staff don't giggle and laugh over something, "because we all see the humor in our existence." He tells the story of the ten-year-old boy whose delaying tactics had successfully warded off an injection for so long that the doctor's patience had evaporated. Finally the clever lad asked, "Are you so old that one minute is that important in your life?" Dr. Martin said, "You bet it is, " and quickly jabbed the boy's butt with a shot of penicillin.

For several years, he savored the misstatements of a local Mrs. Malaprop. "I sent her neighbor to the hospital because she couldn't empty her bladder. A couple of days later, I stopped and asked her if she'd heard anything. Of course, I knew what had happened but I wanted to hear her tell it. She said, 'Yeah, you know they got her up there and they put one of those cafeterias in and took off two quarts of water. That hospital was so busy that they put her right out in the corduroy.'"

Brewster Martin is very aware that he is probably the least financially successful person in his medical school class. He chose this life of the country doctor and would very gladly choose it again. "When I read those nice things writers write about me," he says, "I wonder who they're talking about."

Last and most important, I believe he copes by thinking often of his maternal grandmother, Lelah Elizabeth Davis. From his accounts of her, Mrs. Davis emerges as a strong-minded, pious, music-loving woman of the nineteenth century. Young Brewster Martin—always comfortable around adults—sounds like anything but a modern American teenager. How many kids today would want to grow up in a senior citizen–dominated extended family? And then choose, as adults, to live and work only forty miles from that childhood home and so very far from the bright lights, careers, and excitement of the spots where things seem to be really happening?

In listening to his stories about his remarkable grandmother, I realized anew Chelsea, Vermont's good fortune in having a doctor so steeped in the old-fashioned virtues.

Perhaps it would not have seemed like that to his grandmother herself when Brewster was a boy. One of her favorite admonitions was that life is best if you consciously try to do at least one good thing each day. Young Brewster Martin often went out of his way to do at least one bad thing daily.

My maternal grandmother lived next door to where I was raised in Pittsfield, Vermont. She was a devout Methodist. If we swore in her presence, we were ushered into the parlor and made to learn a verse of a hymn from a Methodist hymnal. After you were able to quote the verse of the hymn, you were allowed to go into the pantry and get a cookie from the cookie jar. As I grew older—I'm not sure if I swore in her presence just to get cookies—I developed this fantastic ability to learn verses of things. I could pick em off in a few moments.

I still sing in the choir and have all my life. Recently some kid said to me, "How come you never have to look at the hymn book?" [*Laughter.*] It's just because I remember all the hymns I learned when I swore in my grandmother's presence.

Brewster Martin

She used to admonish us to try each day to do something good that we were not paid for. In whatever profession we pursued. I still consciously try to do that. Yesterday a paraplegic died here in town. An unbelievably gutsy man—the first paraplegic of the Korean War. Last evening I went to spend a few minutes with his wife. I could have written her a note but I decided that was my little . . . Sometimes it's just a phone call to inquire how someone is I've referred to a hospital. Because people appreciate it. You can't believe how they appreciate that. I'll bet you a nickel that I get a little note from that lady telling me how much it meant to her and her family that I took the time last night to visit. [*He did.*]

Oh, I love people. Maybe I get that from my grandmother. There were always young people around her; I think that's what keeps anybody young. She played the piano and sang. When we were kids, there was never a meal where you didn't go in afterwards and get her to play the piano. When my family is together, we still do. Gosh, they're all very talented. My son-in-law has a master's in performing arts and piano. He's a psychiatrist who can sit down and you'll hum the tune and he can play it. My daughter has a degree in piano; she sings opera in Montreal. I have four kids and they are all musical.

Another gem of wisdom—I call them, nowadays—she used to tell us is that if you look hard enough, you can always see humor in every hour of every day. You can if you are aware of it. Just the other day, for instance, a little kid four or five years old came in with something in his eye. I take hundred of things out of eyes, so it's become routine. You put the anesthetizing drops in and if you can't wipe the object off, then you take a needle to pick it off. I was bent over ready to do it with the needle when the kid reached out and touched my arm and said, "May I ask you a question?" I said, "Yes." He said, "Is this the first time you've done this?" My first thought was, Well, you little brat you. [*Laughter.*] But that's a pretty logical question, isn't it? Kids are great sources of humor.

I have made house calls in all kinds of conveyances. Once in winter the family of a sick man met my car with a dray. That's a horsedrawn vehicle with sled runners in the front; it pulls or drags two poles with boards across them. They took me way back in the hills to where their man was very ill. That old house was just an impossible place to try to care for anyone, so we wrapped him up—it was very cold out—and took him on the dray down over the mountain to the hospital. That dray ride on two feet of snow became an emotional and physical task that I look back on and wonder how I did it. To keep the patient from rolling off in the snow and to keep me and my bag from ending up inside a large snowball required strength I was unaware I possessed.

It's not so bad nowadays, but in mud season in spring the roads would get so muddy that it was impossible to get some places by car. Sometimes I've had to walk in; sometimes I've been taken in by tractor.

One time, early in my practice, I went up in the mountains to see a young woman. According to the neighbor who called, she was having pains in her belly. To get there I had to walk part of the way in. The patient was in a bed covered with a buffalo robe. Do you know what a buffalo robe is? Her mother, who was totally blind, seemed and looked very old. Probably she was my present age. [*Laughter.*] The daughter complained of a pain in her belly and said that for several weeks she'd thought she'd best come up to see me because she thought there was something wrong with the nerves in her stomach. They kept twitching. I asked her if it was a constant pain, or did it come and go.

She said, "Well, it comes and goes."

And I said, "When did you have your last period?"

She didn't know what I was talking about. Finally I asked her when she'd had her last monthly.

She said, "Oh, I don't know. Sometime last summer during haying."

Her mother said, "You haven't had a monthly since last summer during haying?"

She said, "No."

At that point, I threw back the buffalo robe. She was nine months pregnant and in labor.

We walked out of there because I didn't even have an OB bag with me. It was at least half a mile to get to my car. Between pains and contractions, she could walk a few feet. It was her first child. Usually you have a little more time. We got her out to a hospital and did the delivery. She lived such an isolated existence up on that hill that she knew very little about the birds and the bees.

If I had my life to live over again, I would love to be a better pianist. A better parent. I'd love to have been a better doctor. A better Christian. I'm a human being. I think that's the thing people sometimes forget. That I get as tired as they do. I'd like to sleep late some mornings. A lady called me at six o'clock this morning. I didn't get home from the office till 10:30 last night. I just love evenings and to be out walking or cross-country skiing in the moonlight.

If my grandmother were here now, she would probably tell me to reap the most from every day. All through the years, and especially as I get older and older, I find myself quoting her. I found myself quoting her to my own children when they were being reared.

Like I said earlier, she was a devout Methodist. My mother was, too. In April of 1978 my mother died at eighty two. Her Christmas present to each of her four sons was a copy of our family genealogy, which had just been finished. In the front of it, she wrote, "May the good Lord grant unto my children's children's children stout hearts, insatiable curiosity, and an abiding faith. They'll not need more. Love, Mother."

I think that that abiding faith is the thing that really gets me through my worst days. Faith in God and faith that we won't be given burdens we can't surmount. That we'll be given strength and courage to get through the rough days.

So far I have.

"K. E." Mayo

BEEKEEPER

Milton, Vermont
Born: 1909

⟩⟩⟩⟩⟩⟩⟩⟩⟩⟩⟩⟩⟩⟩⟩⟩ ⊛ ⟨⟨⟨⟨⟨⟨⟨⟨⟨⟨⟨⟨⟨⟨⟨⟨

NORTH OF BURLINGTON, IN THE CHAMPLAIN VALLEY, K. E. (Kermit Edward) Mayo is one of those versatile, frugal Vermont farmers who always has a variety of country incomes. In his case, anything from sugaring to trapping to beekeeping.

I met K. E. at the Farm Show in Barre, where he was surrounded by enough honey to stampede a whole county full of bears. He started telling me about his great-uncle. "I used to go over there a lot and the first place I'd head for was the beehive." Naturally I myself had to visit K. E.'s small Milton homestead where at one time he kept as many as two-hundred-fifty beehives. Now he is down to only forty, but he still traps muskrats and produces sugar from over nine hundred taps. He is quite adamant that his soft maples produce better syrup than "that white stuff they make up in the mountains." Sugar or honey, K. E. is a regular at flea markets and fairs.

The subject of change is a pervasive theme of this book. The role of honey in the Mayo family has shifted irreversibly from the old subsistence/barter approach of his great-uncle. That childhood hero apparently did not even *sell* honey, though his cash income was limited to odd jobs in the community.

How I would like to have met K. E.'s great-uncle and to have learned from him about bee trees, sap beer, and honey mead. And how I would like to have interviewed K. E.'s great-grandmother, who was 103 years old when K. E. as a "little tot" saw her. "I can see her now," he says, "sitting in a chair, all dried and wrinkled up, my gosh, and smoking a clay pipe."

If she were with us now, would she agree with her great-grandson that things were better in nineteenth-century Vermont? That's a very important question. But we have run out of shriveled ladies with clay pipes who know the answer.

My grandfather, great-uncles, and father used to hunt wild bees a lot. They used to cut the bee trees late in November, take all the honey, and leave the poor bees to starve to death. So I got kinda soft-hearted. I thought I'd start keeping em.

My great-uncle always had bees, anyway. I used to play around em when I was a kid. I used to go out and stick my finger in some of the honey that was on the outside of the hives. He had the old-fashioned box hive with the top bigger than the bottom and a peaked roof. The frames were in the front and the honey in the back. The bees would put the pollen in the first frames they came to and then the honey frames went the opposite way in the back. That kept the intruders out.

My great-uncle never took any honey away from em because he didn't keep them to make money. The only honey he would ever take would be on the outside of the hive under the roof. When it got crowded inside they'd start putting the honey under the eaves of the hive. When the weather got cold the bees would go inside and leave that honey outside where you could get it without any trouble. And I used to go out there and stick my finger in and eat some of it.

I used to go out and watch his bees. Once in awhile I'd get stung, but not very often. They seemed to like me.

My great-uncle had a white mustache and looked something like Colonel Sanders, except he wasn't fleshy like Sanders. He was tall, skinny. He'd show you anything to entertain ya somehow. He'd even take me down to his shop where he made a lot of things for bees. He used up a lot of lumber making beehives and equipment.

Sometimes on weekends and after school my sister and I would run over to my grandmother and great-uncle's house. It was probably a mile through the pastures and woods. Any time we were missing from the house, my father and mother knew where we were. We wanted to see the different things they had. Bees. An animal in a cage. Like a coon or maybe a mink.

About fifty years ago, when I moved here, I made up my mind I was going to have some bees. We hunted wild bees a lot and found a swarm up on Brigham Hill. I kept the bees in a log out here. Fred Ballard in Milton was an old-time beekeeper and he helped me to get em up from that chunk of wood into a hive.

We cut some bee trees near Colchester Pond. I says, "Let's keep these bees." They acted gentle and nice. Gee, they were beautiful bees to handle. They didn't sting. I brought em home and put em in a hive.

"K. E." Mayo

So I've been keeping bees ever since.

Once we found some wild bees in a cedar tree over here by Lake Champlain. I cut that chunk out in the summer and stood it up next to another tree. It was so heavy and full of honey that I couldn't carry it out then. When our kids went to school in the fall, my wife and I decided to go over and get it. When hunting season starts and somebody runs across a bee tree, they may take it. So we went over to lug it out and, gosh, a bear had eaten it all up. He'd reached in from both ends and eaten all the honey and all the bees.

All bees are domestic. But some people like myself neglect their beehives and don't tend to em and they get crowded and some of em take off. Swarm, they call it. And they'll go to a tree or somebody's chimney or building somewhere. But if you take care of em and give em enough room, they won't swarm.

We claim that honey along the Champlain Valley here is about as good as any you'll find anywhere in the world. Some of the lightest-colored, water-white honey. Well, the light honey is nice to look at but I'd rather have the darker honey myself. I think it's got more minerals, more flavor.

The color gets darker in the fall. In the spring when they first start it's dark, too. You get your lightest honey right around the longest days of the year, around the twenty-first of June.

I like all honey: goldenrod, aster, boneset, motherwort, and all the fall flowers. Joe-pye weed makes good-tasting honey. Dandelion makes a good spring honey but, of course, we don't take off much then cause the bees use it to start rearing their young.

You get forty to one hundred pounds of honey to a colony. Then there might be one or two or three years where you don't get any honey. Due to the season and the flowers they don't get ahead. Some years you have to feed em in order to pull em through.

And if you have twenty hives and somebody puts out fifty across the street, that'd cut your production. There won't be enough bee pasture.

My folks lived off the land and forests. They'd get honey from the wild bee trees and store it up for the winter. Everything like maple came off the place where they lived. Or from right around the neighborhood. Maybe neighbors would swap something and deal that way.

No, they didn't run to the store every time they wanted something. A lot of times we'd go without something like kerosene for the lamps until a certain time when we could get out. 'Cause with those roads we had no way to get out.

Yes, they relied on the land more. Canned their own food. Gosh, when you come right down to it, I think it was better. You didn't have all these things to worry about all the time. Whether an airplane is going to drop on your house during the night while you're sleeping. Or whether somebody's gonna touch off this or that. You were at ease more than you are now.

And they had sap beer and honey mead. That's why they were happier. My great-uncle used to make sap beer a lot out of maple sap in the spring. My father used to make it every year at the tail end of the sugar season when the sap tasted like bud run and didn't make good syrup. When you picked up your buckets, you'd save all that sap and boil it down almost half or two thirds of the way until it began getting quite red. Then strain it and put it in a barrel. Maybe put yeast in to make it work.

It was real powerful. A nice smooth drink which didn't take effect right off. You'd think it was a woman's drink but . . . I remember one night Mrs. Parker came out. She was pretty pious and pretty careful what she did around the neighborhood. My father gave her about six inches of sap beer in a dried beef tumbler. We used to use them as drinking glasses after the dried beef was gone. She always used to go home around nine o'clock. My father gave her this glass. Of course, it was nice and smooth and she sat there drinking it. She kept sitting there and sitting there until 11:30 before she dared to get up off her chair to go home.

But she wouldn't let on. You'd never know.

My great-uncle used to be a great hand to make this honey mead with honey and vinegar. I tried making it a couple of times. You just take some honey and put some water with it and start it fermenting with yeast. Let it work. That's all there is to it. But you don't want to drink too much of it.

Why gosh, why shouldn't anyone become fond of bees? Scientists can't make a comb of honey like the bees can. Only a honeybee can make honey.

Beekeeping just gets in your blood. You get fascinated by em. Well, there's no creature on this earth . . .

I don't call em an insect. Somebody wanted to call them the Vermont insect. I don't want anybody calling em an insect. They're something more than an insect. I call em little heavenly creatures.

Dean McDowell

HORSE TRADER

Sheffield, Vermont
Born: 1896

➤➤➤➤➤➤➤➤➤➤➤➤➤➤➤ ✳ ◄◄◄◄◄◄◄◄◄◄◄◄◄◄◄◄◄

I AM VERY PARTIAL TO PEOPLE who love the animals they work with. In *River Pigs and Cayuses* I introduced a mule-string packer who said of his team, "I don't know. You kinda get attached to em. You hate like hell to have anybody else monkey with em." In Sheffield, Vermont, Dean McDowell had that same affection for his stock. That's what made him a good horse trader.

Most people assume that a successful horse trader is dishonest and full of tricks. Not so, says Dean McDowell. It might just be that he understands that horse better than the other man does. Dean's stories are full of sayings such as "It's all in the hands" and "Use the reins natural."

From the practical point of view, Dean McDowell missed his big chance in life. He began horse teaming at the beginning of the truck era; in fact, the same year the St. Johnsbury Trucking Company was born. But he loved *horses*. Buying, selling, trading, and using them. He points with pride at the matched pairs in the photograph. He names them all and their weights. He remembers using the rightmost white ones to drive twenty miles to fetch a schoolmarm for a dance at Willoughby Lake. Of another team he declares, "When I started in teaming, I had four black horses that would move the earth if you wanted it moved."

His all-time favorite, Old Bill, was a legendary worker: "I've had all kinds of horses in all sizes and I think he was the stoutest thing I ever saw. That horse could pull. He'd move his load or break his rig, one or the other. And I ain't talking about the second time or the third time. The first time you'd ask Bill to pull he would."

Dean acquired Old Bill almost for nothing because his original owner did not understand that if the horse's harness fell down around his rear legs he would kick like lightning. Once, when Old Bill was well past his prime, a busybody named Fred asked about his unlikely reputation as a kicker.

Dean allowed as to how "this horse used to kick a little." The man didn't believe it. "So," said Dean, "I pulled the harness down over Bill's ass and stepped to one side. One heel struck the ceiling on each side of Fred's head. He didn't dodge. He sat right down in the shit and crawled away." [*Laughter.*]

Today Dean McDowell's life is quietly playing out away from the world of teams and trades. But you only have to mention the word *horses* to ignite that old glint in his horse-trading eyes. "If you traded horses, you had to look out. That was all there was to that," he said happily.

My father didn't make a business of it. He traded horses with anybody that came along. He was a farmer and a builder.

He warn't a world-beater. Sometimes he got beat. One summer when I was about twelve years old, he and I hayed on the mountain. He got three heavey broncos and he didn't know that they were branded and he didn't know that they had the heaves. It used

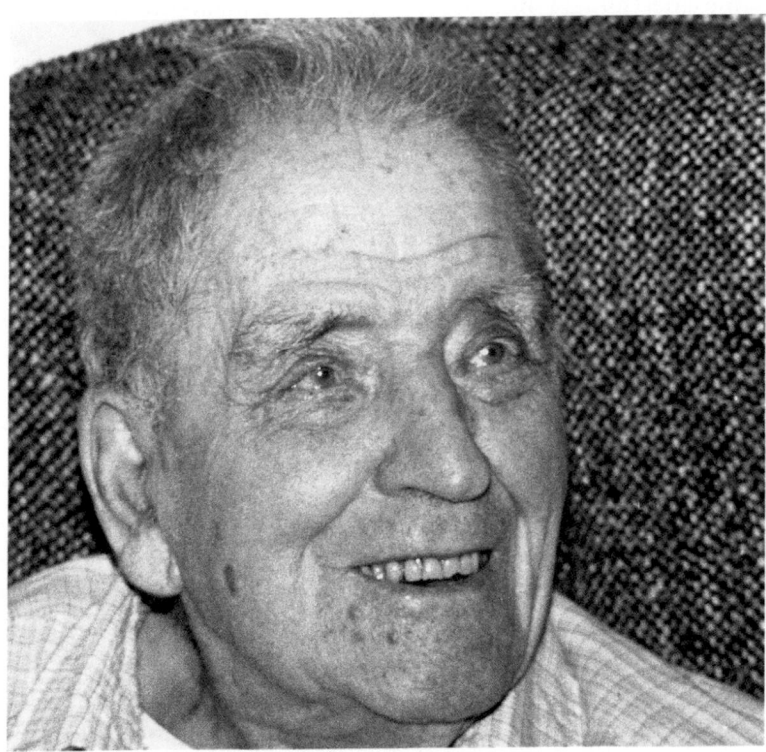

Dean McDowell

to bother him like hell that he couldn't use the biggest one of them at all. But he usually came out better than even.

Yeah, he was good. I learned all I knew about horses from him.

But you've got to have it in your hands. It's the way you pick the reins up, that's all. My boy never drove team hardly any, but when he was a dozen years old he could take a horse that was balky with somebody else and it would pull for him alright. It's just the way you pick the reins up.

You never want to get excited. I warn't more than ten years old when Dad lent my grandfather a mare to use. He lent him the whole rig—horse, harness, and wagon. My grandfather lived in East Burke and we lived in Wheelock and I went over in the spring on the stage to get that rig.

I was coming back and this fella named Frank Chesley drove up behind me. He said, "Have you met any automobiles yet? Is your horse afraid of em?"

Automobiles were just coming out then. God, I hadn't thought of it afore that, but he scared me. I said, "I don't know."

He said, "If you meet any, you get your reins right up in good shape and get your whip out."

By God, he hadn't more than got the words out of his mouth when an automobile came puffing along. Twas a great big red car, a Maxwell; I couldn't have stood on the ground and reached the top of it. Well, I tightened my reins, not fiercely, but I got em up where I could use em good. My mare shied up on the bank a little, but she warn't very afraid. But when I looked over, Frank's horse had turned him around and was headed back to Lyndon with him. He could tell me what to do but he couldn't do it himself.

If there is any reason a horse is going to run away with you, the worst thing you can do is tighten up on your reins. That horse gets everything by telegraph through the reins in his mouth. Don't pull up on em unless you want him to be scared. Use the reins natural.

You might be able to get the better of a man in a horse trade without any planning at all because his horse wouldn't do things for him that it would do for you. As the fella said about training a dog, "You've got to know more than the dog." There weren't any particular tricks to horse trading. Twas the horse that played the tricks. A lot of times there warn't anything the matter with the horse. The matter was with the man that had him.

Traders didn't want to be too dishonest or people wouldn't trade with them. But we thought that anything you pulled over on a horse trader was all right. There was a certain rivalry between traders.

George Cohen was as square a man as I ever did business with. God, you could call him up and ask him about a horse and he could tell you about it over the telephone. If you bought it, it would be just what he told you. That was very unusual.

Steve Gilman was the son of one of them Gilman brothers that kept a sales stable all their lives. My dad was terribly sore at them when he bought a pair of horses there and one of em didn't turn out to be worth a nickel. In World War II, Steve Gilman assumed the business and he warn't no more fit to run it than a goose would be to pray to God. I bought a pair of mares from him for almost nothing. They had each broken about twenty of his halters, but I cured them of that in about a week.

I bought a mare from him for ten dollars right at the beginning of haying. As old a horse as I'd ever seen. I thought somebody'd want her to rake with.

Pete Flanders came to me and said, "If I bring you a man that'll give you $50 for that mare, will you give me half what you make on it?"

I said, "Sure." And he brought Avery Curtis down from Sutton and I sold her to him.

Avery Curtis was a funny combination. He was brighter'n hell. When he was going to the Lyndon Institute he'd carry a stack of books that would drag on the ground. God, he'd get the damndest marks of anybody you ever saw. But he didn't know so much as . . . You couldn't call him an idiot because anybody with a brain like his couldn't be an idiot, but he was pretty near an idiot when it came to trading horses and anything like that.

That old mare I sold him—you wouldn't have given fifteen cents for her. God, she was close to a hundred years old and was just as gray as an old man. But later Avery said that he was perfectly satisfied. "She was not too fast for my other horse," he said, "and she was safe for the children."

God almighty!

Cecil Smith raised ten boys, I guess, in Wheelock. He was a one-horse logger and wrote a lot of poems. "I'm A One-Horse Logger" and so on. I dreamed the other night that he and I met and we were betting about two horses pulling. We bet ten dollars. He had a mare that he used to skid with and I had a roan mare, the one that Dave Smith used to win first prize with once in a pulling contest.

Which one of us won? Well, when you stop to think of it, when I woke up them horses had been dead for twenty years. Warn't much use betting on them. A little too late.

Graham Newell

LATIN TEACHER AND STATE SENATOR

St. Johnsbury, Vermont
Born: 1915

BEYOND INDIVIDUAL ENTHUSIASMS OR HEROES, what everyone in this book is really talking about is Vermont, and not just the geography of a space between the Connecticut River and "York state." The nature of Vermont-ishness is endlessly debatable and fascinating. Certainly this subject always underlies the conversation of former state senator Graham Newell of St. Johnsbury. Senator Newell is both a Latin teacher and a man active in public life, with twenty-six years in the state legislature. He is a person who personifies that quality the Romans called *virtu*, or nobility of spirit.

He is also a seventh-generation Vermonter.

I don't want to make a granite pigeon rest out of him, however. He does have charming eccentricities, like his annual November decoration of Caesar with a triumphal wreath of Vermont ground pine in preparation for an Ides of March pizza party.

His heroes are suitably special, too. You will read about his fascination with Pliny. There was also Cousin Charles, whose influence reached all the way from Paris during the Roaring Twenties, when young Graham was pondering a career as a teacher.

A long-term mentor and friend was the late Blanche Boyer, a University of Chicago Latin scholar. She was a University of Chicago character whose métier as a Latin paleographer was the seventh- and eighth-century Irish hand but who was contemporary enough to cut a black blouse into armbands for her fellow American cruise passengers at the time of Nixon's Saturday Night Massacre. Professor Boyer secured Graham a Chicago scholarship to supplement the money from the sale of his St. Johnsbury bookstore. Much later, after her retirement, she and he made annual trips to Rome where the St. Johnsbury native became a regular at the American Academy and a friend of contessas and principessas. Last winter he accompanied her when she presented the Vatican Library with a hand-bound copy of her latest book, the definitive Latin manuscripts of Peter Abélard.

All this may seem far afield from Vermont and the Northeast Kingdom. Graham Newell, however, is a man who wears his cosmopolitanism as easily as Caesar wears that wreath of "good Vermont ground pine."

I have my great-grandfather Lester Stiles's diaries from the 1850s. I find myself reading them and saying to myself, "There go I."

I was born in St. Johnsbury in 1915 and I'm seventh-generation St. Johnsbury—on both sides of the house, if you please. [*Laughter.*]

Here in Vermont, our culture and our accents are different on either side of the Green Mountains. Even our language—our words and usage—are different here in St. Johnsbury from, say, over in Burlington. On this side, we are geared toward Boston and always have been. My great-grandfather's diaries show that. His thinking was Boston thinking. Whereas on the other side of Vermont, it's Albany and New York City.

I had a Middlebury College roommate who was born and brought up in Middlebury. I was born and brought up over there in St. Johnsbury. We were just as different as could be. He never read the Boston papers. He was brought up on the New York papers. I learned to read on the Boston papers, getting down on the floor on my hands and knees. As a child, Boston was my first city. But he went to New York.

He and I discovered after about a half-year that even though we were both Vermonters our whole perception was different because of those Green Mountains.

The St. Johnsbury Academy was founded in 1842; my great-grandparents attended in 1847 and 1848. In those years education had not become systematized into classes and four-year courses. From my great-grandfather's essays, he obviously was a Latin scholar.

My grandmother was in the class of 1881 and my mother in the class of aught six. They both took the classical course at the Academy, which meant Latin four years and such auxiliary courses as ancient history and philosophy and rhetoric.

What is classical education? Some people think immediately of the study of the Latin and Greek languages. That is not classical education to me. It's more what developed after the Renaissance. Here's an anecdote about what I mean. At the beginning of the whole Vietnam bit, Henry Steele Commager, the historian, made the comment that if LBJ had ever read Thucidydes we would never have gotten into Vietnam. And it's so true. One only has to read Thucidydes's *The Peloponnesian War* and Plutarch's *Lives*. For anybody who reads those, Nixon is back there. There is a Nixon in Plutarch's *Lives*. There were Greeks who thought they weren't crooks, but they were absolute traitors to the cause they represented.

That's what I mean by classical education. One doesn't have to have Latin or Greek to be able to read Plutarch and Thucidydes and Herodotus and the other ancient writers.

At the University of Chicago, I went into the program called the Committee on the History of Culture. In picking a suitable dissertation topic, I came upon Pliny. I studied his letters for what they revealed about his own *humanitas*. *Humanitas* is a word I just won't translate into English because it does not mean our English word *humanity*. To Pliny *humanitas* included everything from benevolence to tolerance to well-rounded-in-culture. Maybe today we'd call it "Renaissance man." I dug out the passages in his letters that reflected his own *humanitas*.

I got so acquainted with Pliny that I still feel as if he were a very close friend of mine. I worked with him almost a year. The more I worked with him, the more he reflected what I would like anybody to say about me.

What got me interested in politics? Vermonters have a love of politics. The town meeting shows it.

I was always running for office. Back in the fourth grade for class office. Class president in eighth grade. And in St. Johnsbury Academy. I was always a politician and I always knew that I'd be in politics in Vermont.

Here in Vermont politics isn't the same as elsewhere. Parties don't mean the same. Jim Jeffords gets elected to Washington by the Democrats and the liberal Republicans. The conservatives hate and detest him. Yet he's there until he runs for the U.S. Senate some day. Over in Montpelier it's a matter of conservative and liberal, not a matter of whatever party has control. Of course, I voted for our new Democratic governor, Madeleine Kunin.

In my book, Bernie Sanders is becoming a good Vermonter because he's so damned independent.

I always called myself a Vermont Republican so I wouldn't be aligned with people like Goldwater. I could disregard them. People would say, "Like whom?"

"Like George Aiken." Now that he has just died, I'm afraid that we're going to make him into a saint in Vermont. Well, maybe that would be a good idea. I notice some people adopting him now whom he himself would totally have ruled out when he was in politics.

Whenever I gave a major speech in the state senate, people expected some erudition. Sometimes I had to produce little quotes for the other senators. All the years I was in the Senate, I was chairman of the Senate Education Committee. They always, with a smile and not at all in derogation, called me the Professor. And some of them knew what my students called me—the Latin name for teacher, which is *magister*. So some of the senators would call me *magister*.

I was on the Senate Judiciary Committee for years; for several sessions I was the only nonlawyer. They always called me the Grammarian in the committee and sometimes on the floor of the Senate. Somebody would get up and ask if he could interrogate the Grammarian.

I insisted upon logical and grammatical expression in the laws. I wouldn't accuse them openly, but many times I felt they were writing little phrases and parts into the law just to obfuscate in order to help their own profession. [*Laughter.*] There *was* some of that, even in Vermont.

In 1953, my first session as a representative, I supported the woman who became the first woman speaker in the country. Later, when she returned to the legislature after the vote, I was the one to give the official greeting. I mentioned how in 1953 the legislature had followed the Virgilian precedent—*dux femina facti*—a reference in the *Aeneid* to Dido's being made ruler of Carthage. "They made a woman their leader."

She's dead now; her name was Consuelo Northrup Bailey. She was a good friend of mine and she'd heard me say this before. [*Laughter.*] She then became lieutenant governor of the state but chose not to run for governor. She didn't think Vermont was ready for a woman governor in 1959.

Latin is always exciting for me because I probably never formulate any sentence without quickly thinking of Latin-derived words. Or the Latin context or how the sentence would sound in Latin. That's the same approach I try to teach my students.

I'm teaching Latin just the same way it was taught to me at St. Johnsbury Academy. I know that the method is a little different than other places because I'm able to cover far more territory. Latin, like most every other course, gets watered down in each generation in the school systems. Latin has gotten down to where some schools cover in two years only three-fourths of what I cover in Latin I. I am still covering as much Latin as I got fifty years ago.

My own method of teaching is amply filled with cultural tidbits. Just this morning, in Latin I, I gave them two phrases. We were talking about some youngster who had to appear in court so I gave them the two phrases *in loco parentis* and *gardien ad litem*. Every day they get three or four such phrases from me.

In loco parentis means in place of a parent. I was using the court as an example. In court someone must be appointed to represent anybody under eighteen.

Gardien ad litem means guardian for this particular case. *Litem* in Latin means lawsuit or strife. Our word *litigation* comes from it.

Early New England farmers knew Latin and the classics well. It's hard to find the reason, but I think it was probably a holdover from the era of the Enlightenment of the eighteenth century. When the New England academy was founded, that was the tradition.

I am aware that people in other states think we Vermonters are unusual. Friends from California have visited me many times. They spend their time here trying to analyze us. They can imitate my speech, but they never can find the answer to what it is that makes us different.

It has something to do with the small town, but there are small towns in other parts of the country.

I think we are intensely loyal. I think a Vermonter is extremely patriotic as a Vermonter. You don't find that in New Hampshire.

When I lived in Chicago, I found that people from the East weren't loyal to their states the way a Vermonter is. I spent one whole day in Athens, Greece trying to trace down a Vermont number plate. To whom it belonged. I finally found out that the original Vermonter had sold the car; it had passed through about four hands and the Vermont number plate was still on it. So it was quite far removed from the Vermonter who had had it.

I'm not one of those who says that you've got to be born here to be a Vermonter. Being a native is not my number one criterion for being a Vermonter.

If you are a Vermonter, you feel like one and you don't have to explain it. If you're talking with somebody else who is a Vermonter, you just know it. [*Laughter.*]   Or to reverse that, if you have to ask what a Vermonter is, you probably aren't one.

Jane Newton

SAWYER

Sutton, Vermont
Born: 1949

━━━━━━━━━━━━━━━━━━ ✦ ━━━━━━━━━━━━━━━━━━

FROM ONE POINT OF VIEW, sawmills are impossibly noisy places where the ears are physically assaulted by the whine of huge saws biting raw wood; by the clunk, creak, crash of conveyors moving logs; and by the snorting of trucks, tractors, and loaders dieseling like ants in an ant nest. From another point of view, a sawmill is a magical place where the mystery of wood's grain, texture, and color is laid bare.

A few years ago, a quietly capable Westminster farm girl named Jane Newton happened upon that beauty and decided to become a sawyer.

Her mentor was Sutton's Warren Fox. He had grown up in sawmills, where his father was a sawyer, at a time when small mills were more numerous than now. He eventually became a teacher after working his way through college in the mills. But he liked his old work, and during summer vacations he operated a small sawmill of his own on Calendar Brook near Sutton. When Jane Newton happened accidentally on the scene at age twenty-four, the middle-aged Fox was beginning to saw year round.

Jane ended up spending eight years helping Warren Fox build up his operation, until going into business for herself with a portable mill. On March 9, 1984, Warren Fox's sawmill burned to the ground.

Jane and three friends — Eileen Riley, Norbert Patoine, and Jim Norris — bought what was left from Fox, installed reconditioned machinery in a new fireproof cinder block and stucco building, and opened for business a year after the fire. They called the new operation Calendar Brook Mill. Undeterred by the economic failure of many other sawmills, they hope to fill a niche for local custom milling of native softwoods like eastern white pine, balsam fir, white cedar, white spruce, red spruce, and hemlock.

Of course, this story could be approached from several different angles, including the three friends' ingenious financing of the mill. But what fascinates me is how a spunky young farm girl came to be a major partner and a skilled sawyer in her own sawmill.

I came here from southern Vermont looking for a change in my life. I came to visit a friend and stopped in to see this sawmill. It was in February 1974, the first year that Warren was sawing all year round. When I came to visit, he had one person working with him in the mill. They were trying to get out an order to which he'd committed himself. The tractor he used as a forklift had just broken a hydraulic hose. He would have to stop sawing in order to fix the hose on the tractor.

Well, I had a car so I offered to fix the hose for him—which I did. I took it to town and got a new hose made up and brought it back and put it on. He didn't have to shut down the mill and he was able to get his order out.

And I had a job.

Growing up on a dairy farm, I'd had an interest in machinery, so it wasn't that difficult to fix the forklift and to drive it and to pick up logs. That was familiar enough not to be a problem. But the whole sawmilling business was totally new to me. I guess I'd gone

Jane Newton

to get sawdust for my dad when I was a kid on the farm, but I never had gotten involved in the process of sawing logs.

When I started working in here, I was bringing in logs and getting to identify the species, the different types of logs. I was just fascinated by the whole process of clamping a log onto a carriage and running it down past this huge saw. And watching the different patterns of the different types of wood come off with each cut. It was fascinating. I don't know why.

Whenever I had spare time, I would stand in there and watch the different patterns of the wood as they opened up. Each cut opened up a whole new sight to be seen.

That fascination stayed with me. I wanted to learn more.

I got so I would help Warren by running the edger to square boards up if they had bark on the outside. When you saw a board off a log, you hitch the log onto the carriage and run the carriage down past this big circular saw. The piece that comes off will often have bark on its outside edges. The edger squares it up to have two straight edges, using two saws that take the bark off. Those saws are adjustable because the width of the pieces you're edging varies according to the size of the log. It was a challenge to be able to eyeball a piece and estimate its width and make a nice square-edged board.

The fascination was not only the different materials coming off the saw and the grain patterns of the wood but also in following that through to the wood's ultimate use.

Warren and I got to know each other quite well in the course of the eight years we worked together building up this business. He never questioned my ability to do most anything. He could have easily thought, Well, she's a girl, she's a woman; better not ask her to do this or better not expect that from her.

He never had that attitude at all, thereby giving me confidence that, sure, I can do whatever it may be. Whether it's unloading a load of logs or fixing a machine that's broken down or carrying my end of a heavy stick. He always trusted me to determine what I could do physically. But never even insinuated that because I was a woman I couldn't do such and such because that was a traditionally male job or role. He was wonderful that way.

I don't know how he came to have that sort of an attitude. Because he did grow up right here in the Northeast Kingdom where roles are very traditional. He never had any children.

He gave me a lot of confidence to go ahead and learn and try.

Most people have accepted me. Oh, there have been some wise guys who try to get a rise out of me. But I don't rise that easily.

Guy Osgood

NORTH COUNTRY GUIDE

Sutton, Vermont
Born: 1907

➤➤➤➤➤➤➤➤➤➤➤➤➤➤➤ ⊛ ◄◄◄◄◄◄◄◄◄◄◄◄◄◄◄◄◄◄

EVER SINCE NATTY BUMPO BLAZED and tracked his way into American litera-
ture, the clever man of the woods has been part of our national cast of
characters. Although for the younger urban generation this man may be
more acceptable as a photographer or wildlife biologist, the lure of the
hunt is still strong in rural states like Vermont. "What I can see, I can hit
at a hundred yards, though it were only a mosquitoe's eye," bragged James
Fenimore Cooper's hero. Less boastful, carpenter Guy Osgood of Sutton,
Vermont, simply told me that "the Osgoods were always great
woodsmen."

Osgood's timber cruiser father's tracking skills reminded me of the
Leatherstocking world where the sound of a carelessly breaking twig
could bring down the fury of Iroquois warriors. The interesting thing is
that his father, born in 1889, was also a minister who preached "strictly the
Bible." I wonder if Reverend Osgood called down divine intervention
against the animals of the godless forest. Or if, like many modern out-
doorsmen, he considered the woods to be a kind of open air cathedral?

In the photograph (front cover), Guy's father—the leftmost man—looks
like an Arctic explorer recently returned from some perilous expedition. (His
distinguished beard disappeared each summer evangelical season.)

That's Guy sitting on the hood of the car, surrounded by his father,
brother, friends, and dead bears. His father's grandmother was a full-
blooded Indian. Although Guy does not know the name of her tribe, he
always says Mohawk "because they were the meanest ones of all." I am
reminded of Henry David Thoreau's travels in Maine with an Indian guide.

The whole business of guiding is reminiscent of the previous century.
Though the chase itself has evolved with improvements in fishing gear and

firepower, it is still the resourceful man of the north woods who maintains mystical ties to the game. Guy says that his father *knew* where the deer were going after he glimpsed them. "Just an instinct," he says. Or was it a skill? And did Guy ever get lost? "I always knew right where I was," he says modestly, "because I knew the country just as well as I know this house."

I was born right up here in Holland, Vermont and I've hunted all over everywhere. I've got ponds that I've been going to ever since 1925. I loved to be in the woods. My father used to take me out when I was twelve, thirteen. I remember I shot a deer when I was fifteen and the deer didn't go down. I run and grabbed him and I got throwed off my feet so quick! It was painful.

If my father ever told you anything, that was it. Of course, he was a minister. He didn't like to go preaching with a beard on so he'd shave it off in the summertime. He went to all the camp meetings, down at White River and all over everywhere. He preached just the Bible. Strictly the Bible. But along in the middle of his sermon he'd talk about hunting and fishing.

Out in the woods he'd show me the different deer and bear signs. Their tracks or where a bear had climbed a tree. Where they were traveling. He'd see a deer sign and he'd say, "Well, that deer ain't been here too long. Maybe half an hour." He seemed to know all of them things.

If my father was on top of a hill, he could holler and you could hear him down below just as plain as if you was standing right beside of him. He'd holler to a bear. You know, a bear hollers just the same as we do. He'd hear a bear holler and he'd answer it. He'd call that bear right up to us.

It'd curl your hair, boy, if you were out in the woods and one hollered right beside of ya. Just if somebody had a woman and was choking her.

I've seen three panthers in this northern country. Once I saw a panther come out of the woods and jump across the road in front of me. He was just as black and had that long tail!

I loved the outdoors so I said, "I guess that's what I'll do." In 1956 I went and asked the big officials up there in New Hampshire if I could get a guide's license. And they said, "Absolutely." They knew me and they knew my father. They knew all of us.

I was with Scott's Idlewild Hunting Camp at Pittsburg, New Hampshire. There was probably twenty of these big hunting camps where the people just flocked in in the fall. Scott was a guide and a fella who had always lived there. Him and his father. He'd probably been guiding for thirty years before I first met him back when I was sixteen or seventeen. He was a peach of a fella.

A good guide will come in and scout the country all over and find out where the deer are. Where they're feeding. Where their runways are.

They eat little sprouts. And they paw a lot for nuts. They love beechnuts. When you see where that deer has pawed under a tree, you've got to be able to tell where he's going. You've got to know the direction he's going to go. If you don't, he'll wear you out before noon.

When a party comes in, you've got to take em out and put em in a good place. Then go around and kind of drive the deer, if you can, to where they can see em. Of course, even then some people couldn't hit a deer.

They were mostly city people. I had a woman once and, boy, was she a peach! She was from Boston and she had that Boston brogue. Boy, I'm going to tell ya, she could hit a deer. She was good. She was good to me, too, and good to have in a party. 'Cause I could put her somewhere and say, "Now you stay right there," and that's right where she'd be if I didn't come out for a week.

I had one fella who was eighty years old. He was always saying, "Stop the ship and let me off; I want to go ashore."

Oh, I had all kinds. Some of em were good and some of em were worthless. You know what I mean. Oh, I used to have some nice ones. Then the next bunch that come in'd be pukes.

You could get a license, too, but you'd want to know the country. They wouldn't like to go out hunting for you every night, ya know. Boy, that's what happens. We had one guide took three of em out. We was a week getting em back to camp.

Also, you've got to get it into your head that you don't want to step on every limb you come to. 'Cause if you do, you'll make more noise that a herd of elephants. So leap right over em and let er go!

I don't doubt but what my father learned something about the woods from his Indian grandmother. But you've got to be out in the woods and really put a study on deer trails and deer tracks. If we jumped a feeding deer, my father could tell ya right where it was going after it had left. He just knew where that deer was going.

He was a regular deer in the woods anyway. He could travel just like a deer. A mile a minute.

And just as still.

Everett Palmer

SUGARMAKER

Waitsfield, Vermont
Born: 1907

➤➤➤➤➤➤➤➤➤➤➤➤➤➤➤➤➤ ⊗ ◄◄◄◄◄◄◄◄◄◄◄◄◄◄◄◄◄◄◄

MAKE NO MISTAKE ABOUT IT. Maple sugar production in the late 1980s is part of agribusiness. In 1984 Vermont led the nation in maple syrup production with 530,000 gallons, valued at $10 million wholesale. Sugar-making is also part of Vermont folklore as a legacy of the Indians and as a local source of sweetness for just about every farm family. Until fairly recently, store-bought white sugar was reserved for special occasions, such as the minister's or school teacher's visits.

Before George Carey came on the scene just before World War I with his Vermont Maple Sugar Company, there was little market for maple sugar products. I was surprised to learn that something now so prized by tourists—and by me—is a newish part of commerce. But then again tourism itself is an equally new phenomenon, spawned by the same roads that make the transporting of bulky, heavy syrup a possibility.

Maybe you imagined a stalwart farmer pouring buckets of drippings into an ox-drawn vat for a sled ride down to a steaming sugar house?

Meet Everett Palmer of Waitsfield, Vermont. A sugarman's sugarman. His tractor long ago replaced ox power; nothing will ever replace the care that annually wins him and his wife Kathryn top prizes at the state farm show. In 1984 they went Best of Show overall for maple products, including blue ribbons for maple cream and for cooked goods.

Newfangled ways have reached deep into the woods. Nowadays, a mountain sugarbush is likely to be laced with a network of plastic pipes. A distant pump aids gravity by sucking the sap from each tree into the line. At the end of the pipelines, a sophisticated osmosis machine simplifies the steamy business of separating the dissolved sugar from the sap.

Everett Palmer and his crew put out 2,500 buckets and use snow shoes to gather the sap. Snowshoeing through the woods with one or two 5-gallon gathering pails cannot be very romantic. I have never done it but

I can appreciate the arithmetic. Since sap is 97.5 percent water and 2.5 percent maple syrup, it takes about 40 gallons of sugar maple sap to boil down to one gallon of syrup. I am a distance walker, but that amount of snowshoeing and carrying sounds masochistic. (And think of all those holes to drill for taps and buckets, or those 45 cords of wood to cut for next season's fuel.)

To me the Palmer's production methods sound like overkill: They empty their sap buckets as soon as only two or three inches of sap have accumulated. They constantly wash their equipment. All this to obtain the best tasting syrup.

One of the Palmer crew, Steve Nikitas, wrote about sugaring in *The Valley Independent* newspaper.

> The sugar house and the boiling down are a treat to behold. First is Mr. Palmer, feeding those four foot lengths into the fire, his face a little blackened and ruddy from the intense heat. Cold sap flows into the evaporator via two holding tanks and a preheater pipe. As it loses its water through boiling, the less sweet sap "chases" the sweeter sap through a series of parallel channels in alternate directions.
>
> By the time it reaches the last section of the last channel, it is syrup. It must be filtered before canning to remove the "niter" which is the sandy substance that makes the wood woody. Then the boiling syrup is tested with a hydrometer to determine its density and thus its grade (Everett produces a lot of the best—light gold Fancy), and sealed in cans.

After detailing the arduous work involved in sugaring, Steve describes the fringe benefits.

> You get to work with fine, good-humored people and there's lots of good-natured joshing and camaraderie amongst all involved. You get to be in the Vermont woods on warm, sunny spring days. You get in great shape. You don't work a routine schedule since the work depends on the sap flow and that varies with the weather. And you get to eat Kathryn Palmer's home cooking.
>
> During those parts of the season when Kathryn isn't up at the sugar house helping out (where she watches and tests the syrup) we are treated to a daily feast, held at noon in the Palmer residence, consisting of meat, baked potatoes, home-grown and canned broccoli, squash, corn, tomatoes, greens, pickles and the like, sweet

rolls, blueberry muffins, the best homemade doughnuts you ever ate and pies for dessert. An array of pies, a different kind each day . . . apple blackberry, cherry cream cheese, strawberry rhubarb, mincemeat or just plain cherry or . . . or . . . or . . .

It is interesting that present-day farm show–winner Everett Palmer at the beginning of his career made sugar cakes "blacker than my boot"; nowadays he strives for the fanciest, most translucent Vermont gold—a preference that is a matter of taste. His southern customers, he says, usually like the darker grades that remind them of sorghum syrup. Champlain Valley Vermonters often tout the stronger flavor of syrup made from their local soft maples. And I have even met one or two benighted souls out West who said that they did not like maple syrup at all. A pox on them!

Like most farmers of his generation, Everett Palmer learned sugaring from his dad, a lister, or appraiser, for the town of Waitsfield. I especially like the story of his father's coming home from work one day to build an arch for his ten-year-old's sugar house. (That's it in the photo behind Everett's steer calves, Star and Bright.)

Vermont has come a long way from the early subsistence sugaring to the major industry that tree tapping has become. But there is one charming folkway that will never change. Have you ever heard of sugar fever? Just observe the glint in any sugarmaker's eyes on the first warm day in February or March. Everett Palmer calls it an urge. He says that "you can tell when the weather feels like sugar weather." I guess that's like being able to tell who is a real Vermonter and who isn't.

That urge must be the answer to why Everett Palmer is still sugaring almost seventy years after he began. "We just like to make the stuff," he says. "It's that time of year and you can't . . ." His voice trails off. No need to explain sugar fever.

Every farmer around here used to sugar. It was an extry income to em. Every farm had a sugar house with six, seven hundred, or a thousand trees they'd tap. There used to be sixteen or seventeen sugar houses in the area. Four or five over there on that ridge when it was all open pasture years ago.

When I was growing up, my dad always sugared. He had three sons and a hired man. During the sugar season years ago, they used to close school for a month. The school board would say, "Well, I think sugaring has come. We will close school down for a month." The farmers would all go to their sugar places and tap. If they had

Everett Palmer

an extry son they didn't need at home, why he'd go and work for some other farmer.

We used to have sugar-on-snow parties. Dad'd encourage me to invite the boys and girls I went to school with in the village. There'd be ten or fifteen come up on a nice day. Mother would sugar off and we'd have sugar-on-snow. Then we'd go to the barn and we'd get them steer calves and the kids would want to drive them. We'd have a good time.

When we were growing up, my dad would have a couple of these young high school boys come help him. The same way when our children were growing up. The wife would have a girl come from another farm and stay with the children when she was up at the sugar house. That's the way we carried on for quite a number of years.

Back in my dad's day, he used to sugar with oxen. They'd weigh anywhere from fifteen to thirty hundred. About every farm around would have a pair of oxen 'cause they were handy to get around in the woods with. You didn't have to use a pair of whip-pletrees. You could bring an ox team right up to a log and put a chain around it. They were stout buggers.

Dad was buying and selling oxen all the time. He'd keep a pair growing up. Younger ones we boys would get handy. We'd raise em up and he'd sell em. Then he'd pick up another pair of calves and raise em up. That was another income.

He was always encouraging me to lead the calves and heifers cause when they got older you could handle em. And we liked to do it.

I trained Star and Bright myself from small calves. You had different-size yokes when they were little.

Of course, my dad didn't tap so many trees as I do now. There warn't that much help and buckets. I can remember that he'd sugar it off and put it into hard sugar and put it into these 25-pound wooden pails with covers that were nailed down. It was sold as hard sugar because of the poor transportation and because there wasn't much demand. Then after that period, Dad used to put it into fifty-five-gallon barrels of syrup and market it that way.

You can tell when the weather feels like sugar weather. It's the air. It's an urge that tells you you'd better be getting up there. I don't know. There's something about it that just puts that feeling right into you. "Well, we'd better be getting up to the sugar place and start in."

Gosh, the old saying was, "It's town meeting time so it's time to begin to sugar." Then another thing they used to go by was crows. When they began to caw in spring people would say, "It's getting to be sugaring time because the crows are around." That doesn't hold now, though, because crows stay around all the time. They didn't used to. I don't know why.

For a good sap run, you've got to have freezing nights and warm days. We'll have maybe four or five such days right along in a row and that's when you get set up. Then after that run, you've gotta have a storm of some kind. Either a snowstorm or rain or sleet. Then have it stay cold for three or four days. Then warm up to 45 or 50 degrees and the sap will run like the dickens. Then you've got to have a storm about every so often to make the sap keep running.

These Vermonters seem to know when it's time to do things like that.

We aren't getting the snow and cold weather we used to get when I was a boy. Lord, you went up there and, why, it would be waist deep.

Yes, my father was proud of me. Well, he didn't ever tell me so, but I was back somewhere when he was telling my mother. I can hear him now saying, "This boy will never starve to death with the way he can handle an axe." 'Cause I used to take and work in the woods cutting my wood for sugaring winters and Saturdays, time off when I didn't have school. He didn't seem to praise me up that much because he didn't want me to get a big head, I guess.

I was very close to my father right up until he died in 1921. He kept me interested in sugaring. He'd just encourage me to keep making this maple syrup. He knew it was keeping me out of the village and getting into mischief.

I've been sugaring ever since I was ten years old. When I first started in, my dad was a lister in town. He and two other men would go around the first of April and list the value of property and people's livestock. For instance, syrup made before the first of April was taxable. Now they don't even tax you for that. They'd always go around and say to the different farmers, "How much syrup have you made before the first of April?" And they'd say, "Well, I don't know; I guess about so much."

After the first of April, you didn't have to pay a tax on it. But we've got records up at the sugar house where we boiled for the first time on the first day of April. It's never the same two years in a row.

I built me a little sugar house right up here at the top of this hill about seventy years ago. When I first started in, I made me a little kind of an arch myself out of some stone. And I had a kettle on it. Just a common kettle. Of course, I didn't have but a few buckets then. And I can remember my mother. [*Laughter.*] She came up and I was keeping the old fire and my face was all smoke and soot. I was having a good time firing it, ya know. Well, she set there and watched me and she said, "I wish, Everett, we could make this thing boil before I go back to the house."

Anyway she must of told my dad about it that night, because the next day he didn't go off listing. He said, "Everett, let's we go up to your little sugar house. We'll see if we can't make you an arch."

He knew where there were two flagstones. They were about two feet wide and about six foot long. They were stacked out somewhere and we went and got em with the old oxen. He had his hired man come help us up at my sugar house. We set em up edgeways.

"Now, Everett," he said, "there are some old grates up on a stone wall," and he told me where they were. I took my steer calves and went up and got em on my sled. They put them two grates in about six or eight inches over the ground so it left a kind of firebox.

Then he remembered a six-foot milk pan. Back years ago when they were shipping milk, they had a room where they would let the milk set to let the cream rise. There was an egg-shaped hole about a foot and a half from the end of that pan where they used to let the milk out.

So he said, "Everett, we've got to solder this hole up." He had his soldering iron in the kitchen stove there in the house. He was pretty handy at things like that. He cut out a piece of tin and he set it into that hole and soldered it in there.

Now he said, "Let's we go up and set the pan on that arch."

And he left a place for the stovepipe. He'd made the arch just long enough so he could set the stovepipe and go up through the roof with it. Then we took some stones and closed in all around the stovepipe. Then we took and mixed up some ashes and made a paste and plastered all around it. Sealed it.

The next morning I started in boiling with that thing. Well, about the middle of the day the frost had evidently come out of the ground, so one of the stones kinda flopped over and a corner dropped down. Of course, I went down to the house crying. Mother wanted to know what the trouble was. So I told her. She said, "There's nothing we can do till Dad gets home."

I can remember Dad coming home. He got the old iron bar and come up and put the stone back in place and braced it so it wouldn't tip over again.

That was my first year sugaring up there. Like I say, that pan was about five foot long. I would boil all day long and I would keep putting sap in. What makes black syrup is to keep adding and you don't take out. I wouldn't syrup off till I got all done at night. Today it wouldn't stand up to thirty-six density because I had no way of testing it. But anyway, I'd take it down to the house. And when mother thought I had enough to make a 25-pound pail, she'd sugar it off and put it in.

I think I made two or three of them pails that year. Then when I got done my dad would say, "Everett, you'd better take your sugar down to Fred Wilder." He was the man who used to buy the sugar. I'd come home thinking I was richer than all get out. Just a few dollars, but at that time I thought it was pretty good pay.

That sugar warn't burnt but twas blacker than my boot. 'Cause I kept pouring in sap while it was boiling away. It didn't make very good stuff. Today, the faster you can get that syrup from them buckets into that evaporator and then get it from the evaporator into that gallon can, the better the syrup you make.

I was the first man here in the valley who put the Seal of Quality on it. You have to earn that. You've got to have a good product. The first part of the season is when you make the nice-flavored fancy syrup. Two-thirds of my crop is fancy syrup.

From the middle part of the season on till the last, I wash out my holding tank, which comes into the sugar house, each noon with boiling hot water. After that there's a difference in the next load of sap. You don't want to let sap set around a great while. I start my men gathering when there isn't only about two or three inches of sap in the bucket. I don't want to let em get full or it won't make that good quality syrup. You want to boil it the same day it runs or bacteria begins to grow. Some fellas will let it run all day today, gather it tomorrow, and boil it maybe the next day. But you've got to boil it the day you pick it up.

When I got out of agriculture school and I came back and farmed, I used to put syrup into barrels and sell it to Carey Maple Sugar Company. People everywhere sold it to these big packers like Carey and it would go up to St. Johnsbury. I sold a lot of syrup for seventy-seven cents a gallon. Now I sell it out of the house for twenty dollars. But you could hire help for little to nuthin back in them days.

How do we do so well at the farm show? Well, there's a flavor that you're looking for. It don't come the first day of your sugaring and it don't come the last day. But it comes in between in the process of sugaring. It's just like anyone else. They don't take and go into the barn and pick the first cow that they got in there and take it to the fair and show it. They take and pick out one that they figure is the better animal.

If I could bring them buckets in in the middle of the season and wash em and put em back out again, I'd make still better syrup.

My help will tell you that I'm a fussy cuss. But quality is what we want and I try to make the best syrup that I can make.

William "Bud" Pearl

GRAVEDIGGER

St. Johnsbury, Vermont
Born: 1921

⇢⇢⇢⇢⇢⇢⇢⇢⇢⇢⇢⇢⇢⇢⇢⇢ ⊛ ⇠⇠⇠⇠⇠⇠⇠⇠⇠⇠⇠⇠⇠⇠⇠⇠⇠⇠

WHEN I VISITED THE MOUNT PLEASANT CEMETERY in late January, cross-country ski tracks laced across the hillside of tombstones. This graveyard is used in winter by skiers as well as in summer by joggers and strollers. That would have pleased the founders of one of Vermont's oldest cemetery associations. In 1850 they chose the Mount Pleasant site above St. Johnsbury for its tranquility, beauty, and good digging.

Inside the cemetery office, Bud Pearl, raconteur gravedigger, served me a lunch of corn fritters slathered in maple syrup from his own sugarbush. He was a handsome man, as imposing as a Roman bust or a Vermont granite statue. He wore dark glasses with horse blinderlike side panels because his corneas had been ruined by years of staring into the crematorium's flames.

Bud Pearl is a man accustomed to death. He was born on Bennington Day, 1921 — long enough ago that his epitaph-sprinkled talk is like a walk through a Victorian cemetery. Bud knows stories about most of his residents: "I'll tell you about a man buried down here that my father worked for at the E. T. Fairbanks Company. He was a very sensitive man, very much aware of the life around him. He wrote a book of poems as a tribute to his wife, who died before her time. To me this poem expresses quite remarkably his sorrow over the death of his wife and yet his appreciation for her.

> The stars have fallen from the skies.
> A cloud obscures the sun.
> A veil is drawn o'er earth's fair form
> My day of joy is done.

"That was written by Charles H. Horton and I think of it every time I go by his grave."

He fetched me a glass of water from a pitcher he kept in the ever-cool tomb. I walked back there with him and was surprised to see a miniwarehouse of caskets waiting under the arched ceiling for spring thaw. If you die in Vermont in winter, you must wait until about April for burial.

In response to my questions about heroes, Bud talked mostly of his Aunt Lillian. Her mission had been to visit her church's parishioners representing their otherworldly minister. In the 1980s she would have become a minister herself. Bud described her as a maiden lady and the type of aunt everyone should have. Someone who had an obvious joy in seeing him. "My aunt went about doing good," he said, "and she was a light along the way."

Her untimely death and the lingering early death of his father from a stroke were "terrible experiences that make you aware of what can happen." Combat service in World War II sharpened that sense of loss, as did daily work at the cemetery.

But Bud Pearl is far from morose. His irresistible sincerity and Vermont humor made me feel right at home in the graveyard. It *is* a personal place. For instance, unlike other crematoriums, Mount Pleasant never reduces the deceased to numbers in the death-to-ashes process. "We think that life is too full of numbers," says Bud gently, "to put a number on someone's casket instead of their name." I admitted that I hardly ever think about cemeteries. "That's right," Bud laughed.

Bud is what he would call an old-fashioned Christian gentleman. The stories he told me were often emotional stories, emotionally told. I still remember the deep conviction with which he said, "She put out good and it rested with a great many people. I'm sure that one's memory of that helps one to go on. It has to! It has to!"

Life at Mount Pleasant engenders a special perspective. When I had finished my fritters and syrup, Bud said, "I think you are constantly reminded here in the cemetery that the things that are seen are temporal and the things that are unseen are eternal."

"What else *can* you think?"

I am a professional gravedigger. We take pride in our graves here. We dig good graves. When we get done, they look as if they've been cut out with a cheese knife. They're hand dug and they're good, deep graves. I've stretched out in the bottom of a lot of graves here and said, "This is a good grave and it'll be comfortable."

William "Bud" Pearl

Depending on the condition of the ground, we can put a grave out in two-and-one-half hours. A couple of men with shovels. That means cutting out the sod and putting it to one side and digging out the dirt and putting some aside because it's going to be taken away. The dimensions are roughly seven feet long and thirty-four inches wide. Between five and six feet deep. Afterwards we fill the grave and we tamp around the box and on top and we put the sod back. We've had a lot of people come up later and want to know where the grave was.

That's the way to do it. Make it look as if you'd never been there.

I have to talk with people who come up here to the cemetery, usually on a sad errand. My aunt, too, used to talk to all manner of people; she spent a large part of her life being the official church visitor for the North Church here in St. Johnsbury. She called on people and kept the minister in touch with people in the parish about sickness or whatever. Auntie called on all manner of people. There was a brother and sister. His name was Blake. He used to have oranges to sell and they called him "Sweet and Juicy" because he always talked about his oranges. He was not very clean. Anything but. There was quite a lot of dirt around their house. But my aunt used to call on them. She called on everybody.

At the annual meeting, people would give all these lengthy reports, and Aunt Lillian would get up and say very quietly that she had made over a thousand calls in the parish during the past year. She didn't pick or choose. She called on everyone regardless of whether they were over to the poor farm or where they were. She was a wonderful human being.

The minister she helped—the one I admired so much—was a scholar. He was a wonderful speaker. He spoke in church on everything from the Bible to Savonarola to the League of Nations to the works of Shakespeare. He was perhaps the best-educated speaker who ever resided in St. Johnsbury. If people could hear him today, they wouldn't believe that he spent sixteen years here.

But he was not a practical man. He could go from here to Danville in his car and never get it out of second gear. His mind was off in other places a great deal of the time. He was a very kind man, but going around visiting was not his forte. It just wasn't. But if my aunt relayed to him something she thought he needed to look into, he did.

He was a Christian gentleman from the word go, but his whole life was geared to his mind and his command of the English language. I've seen him stand on street corners in the cold and wind with his hat in his hand when he was talking to a lady. It was just as natural to him as it would be for you and me to take a step.

He was very well traveled. He was born in India, the son of missionary parents. He always wore pince-nez glasses. In church he wore a robe. He put so much into his sermons that during and after he would pull out a handkerchief and wipe his brow and take his glasses off and wipe around. He put so much into it every Sunday. Just incredible what that man did here. And, of course, there were people who thought he talked over their heads. I always felt they could reach out a little bit.

His name was George Avery Neeld. He was one of the finest men that I've ever known anywhere.

One of the things about my aunt and about this minister was that they never had any thought of gaining anything for themselves. In money or power or influence. He made you think about what a lot of things were leading up to. He could see that the failure of the League of Nations would be a disaster for the world.

My aunt died soon after I went into the service in 1942. I was in uniform and that troubled her, of course. She didn't want to think about war. That would be entirely foreign to her.

I can tell you just exactly where I saw my aunt last. At the close of her life, she suffered from acute depression. It was a physical thing in her head, I suppose, but it left her dangerously depressed. There wasn't a great deal they could for her. The last time I saw her,

I went over to the state hospital in Waterbury where she was a patient. I went into her little room and visited. She was tickled to death to see me; that particular day she didn't show any symptoms. People would come by the door—there was no one there who was violent—and peer in to see what was going on. I was in Army uniform at the time.

When it came time for me to leave, she walked with me to the door. I can see her now waving and smiling at me from the confines of that institution. It's a memory I shall never forget. She didn't live long after that.

It's a peculiar thing about life. When I was a boy, I used to be very interested in the generals of World War I. I could tell you all about Maréchals Foch and Joffre and Pétain and Ludendorf and Hindenburg. I took great delight in reading about them. And the Russo-Japanese War and all that sort of thing.

But when I came to take part in a war, I found out it was entirely different. I think about one boy in particular who died over in the Pacific. Theodore Spotted Bear came into my platoon. He was an Indian boy from Oklahoma. His people lived on a reservation. He was eighteen years old. I thought he was kidding when he gave me his name, but it turned out that he wasn't. He was with us for a few weeks and was a fine boy.

Then one day he was as near to me as you are and he was shot right in the forehead. He never grunted; he never moved; he never said anything. He was dead. In a few weeks it'll be forty years ago that that happened.

After you have something like that happen and many other things of that kind, why all the glory of General Foch is gone.

I think that my aunt's life could be summed up in a few words: Good diffused may more abundant grow. She put out good and it rested with a great many people. I'm sure that one's memory of that helps one to go on. It has to! It has to!

Although you may grieve over the death of a friend or family member, the paramount thing when death occurs is that something must be done with the body. It *has* to be done. You have to face it; there's no other way. So you do the best you can, though you are very upset. But the job has to be done.

A few days ago I cremated a good friend of mine. Her name was Elizabeth Vickery. We used to call her Trader Vic. She was a train buff and her favorite ride was to go from Montreal to Vancouver. She thoroughly enjoyed it. In fact, she's been known to go twice in the same year. The train crew got so that they knew her and welcomed her aboard and she, of course, got a great kick out of that.

My wife Lucia pretty much looked after her in the last years of her life. She had a remarkable outlook on life. She said, "I'm ready to go anytime; I've had the good part. It's all downhill from here on and I'm ready to go anytime."

She wanted cremation when she died, with her ashes to be buried here at Mount Pleasant. She was brought here for cremation just a few days ago. When I placed her in the crematory I closed the door and said, "Last train to Vancouver, Trader." And I cried.

I guess anybody would who knew her. She was a wonderful human spirit. When she'd laugh, she'd jiggle all over. Trader Vic!

Of course, if you want to die in Vermont, you want to die in Ely, Vermont, because you can get a very nice funeral there from Bill Godfrey for hundreds of dollars less than you can other places.

Did you hear the story about the lady he went to see when her husband died? When he went to the house to make the arrangements, she kept wiping away the tears with her apron. Finally he said, "Well, I guess we've covered everything, unless you'd like me to get you some flowers?"

"Flowers! Flowers!" He said she put that apron down and her whole countenance changed. She said, "I'll tell you, he warn't no flowers to live with."

She wasn't about to buy any flowers for him. [*Laughter.*] Oh, Bill would laugh over that. He's a corker.

I guess my heroes are family heroes. They are always in the background of my thoughts. Sometimes in the foreground. They have influenced me a great deal.

I have tried to live in a way that my aunt would be as proud of me as she was when I was a boy. That's probably asking more than I can do.

She was a ray of light to everyone she met. There was no meanness in her. She shed a great deal of hope and joy wherever she went. I haven't matched that, but I hope that at least some of the time I have been worthy of her.

We're very fortunate. We have good earth here. What we call good digging. Glacial till — the bottom of a glacial lake. We use no backhoes, no machines. It's all hand dug.

Well, why not? We're here and we can dig em, so we do. [*Laughter.*] Yeah. And you don't have anything running over the lots breaking up things. We're quite proud of that.

It's a source of satisfaction. We know that what we're doing needs to be done. The chances are it's rather permanent.

Belle Perry

QUILTMAKER

Waterbury, Vermont
Born: 1891

➤➤➤➤➤➤➤➤➤➤➤➤➤➤➤ ⊗ ⊰⊰⊰⊰⊰⊰⊰⊰⊰⊰⊰⊰⊰⊰⊰⊰⊰

BECAUSE BELLE PERRY IS ALMOST one hundred years old, she can remember when the usefulness of quilts was not primarily decorative. "We lived in cold houses," she says and I believe it.

Belle Perry's eyes and fingers aren't what they once were, but she is happiest when quilting at her little house in Waterbury. When I asked about her hero, she unhesitatingly said "my mother." Like her mother she worked hard all her life, first raising a family under arduous circumstances and then laboring as a nurse, though she could never afford a nursing degree.

Belle Perry's mother apparently had that strain of doughty resilience I detected in Belle herself. Certainly as far as quilting went, like mother like daughter. "I kept agoin by her'n," she says of the way she originally learned quilting.

To find beauty in remnants and castoffs is no small thing.

Belle showed me how to make the flower design of her long-ago original quilt. Out came a series of four-color, eight-piece rounds which she handstitched upon a white background with black embroidery thread. The effect was of a field of flowers. She said, "They make the prettiest bedspread you ever saw in your life."

In one breath Belle Perry talks of her prayers and her cemetery plot. In the next, she shows her old spunk and says, "I ain't dead yet and I'm goin to keep asewin as long as I can."

Oh, good God, I started when I was fourteen. I've made hundreds of em. I sold nine tops to one man the other day here.

I'm going to show you how I sew this big flower onto the white background. There's a hole under this fingernail just like a thimble. And when I get my needle in that hole, then pull it out, then I've got a stitch took. Then I go back gain and go through the cloth to my fingernail. At first it hurts awfully till that hole heals up.

I started in same as my mother did and kept aworkin em up. I kept agoin by her'n and I thought that I could make a little mite better-looking one. And I saved my pieces and put em together to see what would go good together and what didn't. And I kept adoin like that.

I trace my pieces out on a piece of cardboard. Here's my pattern for a bow-tie quilt and here's a flowered one for a bed quilt.

I used to use everything. The neighbors had a lot of family and they used to make their own baby clothes. They used to give me the little pieces. I saved every little piece. What didn't go into one quilt went into another one.

There are 101 ways to put a quilt together, but the most important thing is to sew em good and to get good cloth. I used to use everything for cloth. Thin and light and thick and thin. Because I had a big family and my mother died.

I used to watch my mother do it and that's how I caught on. I thought she was the best woman who ever lived. We never got much education, just fifth grade, that's all. But she did the best she could. She was a very pleasant woman. Good to everybody. Wanted to help everybody. My mother and my grandmother, they was all great workers.

The houses were cold because they had to burn wet wood in a great big, tall old-fashioned stove. All I had was a regular box stove. You couldn't bake on it. All you could make was pancakes on top of it. We took some flour and a little lard and if we didn't have no milk to mix em up with, we mixed em up outa water. I tell you, boy, it was hard times.

I used to go in the woods and help my husband cut logs for firewood. Our horse would keep awalkin to make the saw run.

We sold baskets and people used them for everything. Clothes baskets. Lard baskets to put lard in when they butchered. Sixty-six years ago my father dropped dead out in the dooryard pounding ash offn a log to make up some baskets.

My mother died just six months and four days after my father died.

When I was fourteen, I gave the first quilt I ever made to my mother. Back then I thought I knew it all. I wasn't any different than any other young person. She saved it and gave it back to me after I was married. Then I saw that I didn't know as much as I'd thought. I kept againin on it, but I don't think anybody could beat my mother's quilts. I guess I think that because she was my mother.

I'll make any design that anybody wants from a teddy bear on up. Mostly I sell these flower designs.

Oh good gracious Peter, I made a lot of quilts in my day.

L. Henry Potter

NATURALIST

Clarendon, Vermont
Born: 1891

➤➤➤➤➤➤➤➤➤➤➤➤➤➤➤ ⊙ ◄◄◄◄◄◄◄◄◄◄◄◄◄◄◄◄◄

AT HENRY POTTER'S OLD FARMHOUSE, the talk often turns to chromosomes, to hybridization, and to hybrids becoming fertile by doubling their chromosomes and mating with their parents. No, Henry's not talking cows, though he is a retired dairy farmer who plowed with oxen as recently as 1945. The subject is ferns, the five to six hundred species growing north of Mexico and especially the sixty six native to Vermont.

Did you know, for instance, that the maidenhair spleenwort grows on ledges?

Much more than most people, Henry Potter has lived a life of great continuity. From this same house, his great-grandfather used to set out with a two horse team to take his cheese to Boston "over the height of land before they built this railroad." Henry himself has long visited that railroad's Summit Cut on that same height of land to search for rare ferns. For him the continuity of human associations and the endurance of natural patterns is an everyday reality and source of strength.

Originally he learned about nature from his parents and then from older naturalists. Sometimes he published the findings of his many field trips as botanical notes, but his contribution has been primarily as a teacher. He is an inspiration and a link to the world of distinguished nineteenth-century naturalists.

Of course, a comparison suggests itself with that other naturalist named Henry who died three decades before farmer Potter's birth. Thoreau was a canny observer of nature's external manifestations: the colors of leaves, the passage of the seasons, the habits of the animals. But his untimely death from consumption at age forty five cut him off from the revolutionary advances that were about to transform natural science. Darwin's *The Evolution of Species* was not published until 1859, shortly before Thoreau's death in 1862.

Henry Potter's favorite natural history writer is John Burroughs, another figure active at the dawn of contemporary science. The value of Thoreau, and Burroughs, and Henry Potter, it seems to me, is not the specific natural history content they communicate but their attitude toward the nonhuman world. Their reverence is not a complex thing. You can see it in the face of the young girl who is learning about ferns from the sage of Clarendon. You can see it in Henry's own eyes when he reminisces about his favorite field trips.

Henry Potter is an old dairy farmer whose clothes show the labor of frugal bachelor mending. He wears his honors as naturally as a fawn wears its spots: Vermont Naturalist of the Year, from the Vermont Institute of Natural Sciences; Vermont Chapter Award from the New England Wildflower Society; and Doctor of Science from the University of Vermont. The citation for the latter degree, which Henry received in 1981, reads:

> He attended a nearby country school through the ninth grade. Careful observation and a good ear soon made him a respected field ornithologist. A gift of Gray's *Manual of Botany* applied to plants in his father's haymow on slack winter days taught him the terminology and complex identification processes of the field botanist.

Money, fame, and advancement rarely accrue to amateur naturalists. None of these are necessary when internal rewards are so great. "I've been intensely interested all the while," he says. "By the time I was grown up, I was pretty well versed in nature."

Enthusiasm and dedication are their own rewards. Henry remembers scaling a nearby cliff to film a nesting falcon. His attempts to photograph skunks sometimes ended in smelly failure. He showed me a scrapbook of box camera photos of skunks, mice, owls, red squirrels, beavers, woodchucks, flying squirrels, and deer — deer walking and running and looking surprised. "A fox went by here," laughed Henry, handing me an old picture which was embarrassingly bad. "Kinda fast. Really fast, like a blur!" My ninety-four-but-young host dug through the pile of photos looking for his favorite shot, while we laughed and laughed. "Here's the one I was looking for. You see, down through there I saw a doe with her little one in the morning. My brother Arthur and I were milking. I got my old Graflex and I went down there. She saw me coming and she went right down through the barway. The fawn had been playing; pretty soon he looked up and he didn't see his mother. 'Maaa,' he says. He saw me there and came right up to me. So I took his picture." [*Laughter.*]

I asked him if he was religious in the church sense. He said, as I expected, "No, not especially. But I've got nothing against religion. When I'm out in the woods, I think about how all these nice things came about. And how great it is. But I studied Darwin early and, of course, I don't believe that we humans came here all at once. We evolved is what I figure.

"But just the same there's something that makes this thing work. Some power of some kind. There is something back of it that makes things tick."

I was a dairy farmer all my life. My parents and my three brothers were all interested in nature. We were out in the fields every day and we had a chance to see those things. We enjoyed it. I was inspired at an early age.

Later on in 1910 I joined the Vermont Bird and Botanical Club. I met a lot of naturalists and got started in botany and birds and started a little botanical collection of pressed specimens. All the plants at first, but some years ago the American Fern Society met nearby in Wallingford and I took them afield to show them ferns. That's when I got especially started on ferns.

I was born in Wallingford, the next town over to the southeast here. My parents had a small farm there. This farm here was owned by my great-grandparents. My father bought this place and I moved here when I was seven years old.

I used to go afield with my father and my mother. She was interested in flowers and plants. He was especially interested in animals. The first bird song I remember was the veery thrush, when I was five years old. Dad called em swamp robins. One day after chores, he and I went out on a little hill overlooking an alder swamp and we heard that song. My first bird! [*Laughter.*]

My mother's father was an old-fashioned botanist who knew all of the local plants' medicinal properties. I remember going along the hedgerows here with him as he told me what the different ones were good for. Oh, they used to gather catnip and smartweed and spearmint. If you were coming down with a cold, you'd make a bowl of catnip tea and go to bed. Spearmint I think was for fevers.

My brother Eddie was seven years younger than I was and he took to this nature study the same as I did. He and I used to photograph these drumming grouse in the spring. We used to put up a blind and stay in there all night and be there when he started to drum. We'd pull a string to fire the camera's flashbulbs.

We had a lot of older botanists in the Bird and Botanical Club. Dr. Brainerd was a famous botanist. He was a Middlebury man. When they'd have their annual field meeting, he was a natural teacher. He would take particular pains to instruct a young man like me on the different plants. He was a great violets specialist and wrote a book on them. At one time, he had all the violets of North

L. Henry Potter

America growing in his garden. I remember that once we had a meeting up north in the state and Dr. Brainerd came along. He got out probably half a dozen plants he'd collected. He said, "Henry, how many of these violets can you name?" It happened that I named all of them. He looked at me and said, "You've been studying my violet book." [*Laughter.*]

Here's a picture of me and Frank Dobbins in York state at a nice little waterfall. John Burroughs is buried there in the Catskills. He was my favorite author because he talks about the everyday things you've seen yourself. You can feel you're right there by reading his books.

I knew Harold Goddard Rugg very well. At the Bird and Botanical meetings, he always went afield; he was a great botanist from Dartmouth. Quite a long time ago, somebody collected a fern in Connecticut and sent it to him. They thought they had a new species of fern, but he said it was a hybrid between the royal fern and the interrupted fern, which are both common ferns here. Well, they got to growing that fern in different places and the experts determined that he was right and so they named it *Osmunda ruggii.*

I've been noted as a fern man lately, especially hybrids. They are rather interesting because a hybrid will have characteristics of both its parents. Here in Vermont, we have sixty-six distinct species and over twenty hybrids. Lately I've been working on getting out a little pamphlet on these hybrids. My pamphlet won't be technical at all because I don't believe in that so much. If you were just starting in on ferns, you wouldn't want a lot of this chromosome business.

Ferns are especially enjoyable. The more you study them, the more interesting they get. Take the *osmundas*, for instance. They're different from all the other ferns because the root system of the *osmundas* produces what I call fairy rings. Their roots branch out in various directions. At the end of each root, they produce another plant. They go a few inches every year and finally you have a ring.

Osmunda is the genera name. We have three species here: the royal fern, the interrupted fern, and the cinnamon fern. They all have that same habit of spreading out. That root system is down deep enough so that if a forest fire should come through, it won't kill the ferns. They'll come right up again.

Osmundas grow a deep root system, but some others grow right along on the leaf mold. Some grow on rocks. Some want acid soil, some want limestone, some want sandstone. As you study them, it's interesting to see the different habitats they grow in.

My hearing is still good. I can go out here in the summer and listen and know all the birds that are nesting. Studying nature helps you to stay young.

I joined the Vermont Bird and Botanical Club in 1910. It still exists today, but it isn't what it used to be because there aren't so many active botanists anymore. The older people are gone. I miss them; they had a lot of good information.

The young people don't seem to take it up. Maybe their parents don't start em on it when they're young. That makes quite a difference.

Greg Renner

EARTH SCIENCES TEACHER

Bradford, Vermont
Born: 1950

➤➤➤➤➤➤➤➤➤➤➤➤➤➤➤ ✷ ◄◄◄◄◄◄◄◄◄◄◄◄◄◄◄◄◄

PINKIE MUST HAVE BEEN quite a teacher.

I do not know if he was the popular type high schoolers dedicate their yearbooks to. Somehow I picture him as a florid man whose enthusiasms touched few students. But Pinkie made a great difference to one former Massapequa High student named Greg Renner.

Today Greg teaches Earth Science at Oxbow High School in Bradford, Vermont. My visit to his classroom was too brief to answer all my questions about rocks, clouds, and seas. I envied his ninth graders their chance to sample his natural history of the surface of the earth—its crust, land forms, atmosphere, and oceans, the place of the earth in the cosmos. "It's a broad subject," said Greg, "and the teacher has a lot of latitude in what he can cover."

A teacher like Pinkie is a very special hero to the student whose life he or she changes. I like the image of the Olympic runner passing a flame to the next person in a relay. Teaching at its best is that kind of hand–off. "A teacher has to be a role model, too. If you're not in love with your own subject, it's very difficult to get other people enthusiastic about it," Greg said. "One of the teacher's prime goals is to instill the interest in self-learning that adults must have to lead intellectually productive lives."

His last name was Kritzberg. I believe his first name was Arthur, but the kids called him Pinkie. He was a red-haired gentleman with a flushed complexion.

When I was a ninth grader, full of energy and with more than my share of mischief, I found myself in his course, called earth science. At first I found it *somewhat* interesting.

But the more Pinkie taught us, the more interested I became. I noticed that he was the kind of person who had a tremendous amount of joy, a real sparkle in his eyes when he was describing some of the trips he'd taken out West, climbing Mount Rainier, et cetera. He always brought back a bunch of slides to show the classes. Most of the kids were somewhere between amused and bored, but I was totally interested in all the things he was telling us about.

I thought it would be kind of neat to do something like that. To take the aspects of the world I found interesting and to make them into a career. It didn't dawn on me then that I would become a teacher, but the memories of that experience never left me.

I was a psychology major in college. After I came out of the service, I decided to pursue a different type of career. My memories of the joy that fellow had had, the sparkle in his eyes, really stuck with me. I thought it would be something I'd like to try.

Pinkie was not a superhero or someone larger than life but rather a very down-to-earth individual living an ordinary life. He really did make an impression on me. He wasn't heroic because of any great feats he'd done but because he seemed to truly enjoy and be satisfied with what he was doing.

The classes of kids he had to deal with were pretty demanding on his patience. I wouldn't be surprised if toward the end of his career as a teacher he felt burned out at times. But I didn't see any symptoms.

A teacher has to recognize and avoid the symptoms of burnout. If he's working too hard and it's taking its toll, he's simply got to put the brakes on for awhile and find some diversions. I think this is a case where the tortoise wins out over the hare. If a person is interested in teaching as a lifelong career, he *can't* burn out after three years. He's got to find some way of coping with the stresses and enormous work loads that a truly dedicated teacher will assume for himself. Durability is important. A durable teacher knows how to pace himself without losing enthusiasm for the job.

If you don't love what you're doing, you wouldn't be a teacher. The financial rewards are not that great. You do it for other reasons than financial gain. I think Arthur Kritzberg understood that. [*Laughter.*]

You need a very personal approach. If you are too pedantic, you can spend your time in front of a classroom talking to faceless, nameless bodies just to transfer information. Without a more personal way, that method is very boring. But when you realize that your students are all individuals with different personalities, different learning styles, and different attitudes . . .

Of course, they go through their own adolescent crises from day to day. In a class of twenty-five kids on any given day you're going to find a whole range of stresses, attitudes, and moods. You simply have to get involved with them as individuals if you're really going to be effective in teaching them and arousing their curiosity about the sciences. That's where a lot of the rewards really come.

The modern teacher tends to be somewhat of a generalist. I've always been surprised at how many of my colleagues have come to teaching from other professions and training.

I think what makes a good teacher is not necessarily the amount of background course material in his or her subject area, although that is important. I think probably the most important aspect of being a successful teacher is the ability to communicate knowledge to other people. Packaging and marketing the knowledge and enlivening the student's curiosity require certain personality traits to be successful. It's a skill you can't learn in any college.

After I had been teaching earth science for several years, I attended a teachers' convention in Hartford, Connecticut in 1978. Much to my surprise, I recognized a teacher there who was a member of the staff of my old high school. I asked him if Mr. Kritzberg was still around. He said, No, that he'd retired but that they were still in touch. I asked him to go back and tell Mr. Kritzberg that there was at least one student in his career who admired him for what he was doing and who became an earth science teacher like him.

I hope that the message did get back to him. One of the things I find most satisfying is when students come back—particularly students I'd felt were not especially promising—and tell me that my class reached them in some special way or contributed to their success or career choice in later years.

When my former twelfth grade physics students come back from college, we sit down and talk about how my course prepared them for college. It's always interesting to see how some students, who I never thought were skilled in physics, have gone on to become physics majors or engineers.

It's taught me that you can never sell a kid short. The ones you feel will be least likely to succeed are often the ones who turn around and surprise everybody.

That's one of the things that keeps a teacher going.

Charles B. Ross

MORGAN HORSE BREEDER

Hinesburg, Vermont
Born: 1920

> �廾廾廾廾廾廾廾廾廾廾廾廾廾廾廾 ⊗ 廿廿廿廿廿廿廿廿廿廿廿廿廿廿廿廿廿廿

CHARLIE ROSS IS A RETIRED FEDERAL APPOINTEE who spent many years in Washington, D.C. before returning to Vermont. His twin passions—Morgan horses and public service—evolved out of family roots in the Green Mountain State. "When you've been brought up in a small country town in Vermont," he says, "particularly when both sides of your family have lived in Vermont since the late 1700s, you're bound very strongly to the soil and to the outdoors and to animals and self-sufficiency."

Although I knew that the Morgan horse is the Vermont state animal, I was not aware of how much it has influenced several sectors of American horse breeding. Of course, Morgans have been dominant in the horse family called standard bred, comprising trotting or buggy horses. But an offspring of Justin Morgan was also a founder of the saddle bred show horse registry. Yet another offspring helped found the quarter horse registry. What speed, strength, and prepotence Justin Morgan must have had!

A frisky Morgan at work is a sight to behold. Imagine the beauty of two Morgan-pulled sleighs crisscrossing the grounds of the state capitol in honor of Governor Kunin's inauguration: erect heads, prancing feet, blowing manes. The sleighs were an extra Vermont touch the new governor wanted for her big day.

And that's how I met Charlie Ross of Hinesburg's Taproot Morgan Horse Farm. For me the place and the event combined nicely to showcase Charlie Ross's interests in horses and government. Charlie is not a famous Vermonter; he never held statewide office and his 1974 U.S. Senate bid was unsuccessful. But service as a Burlington city alderman and then as chairman of the Vermont Public Service Board led to a Kennedy appointment to the Federal Power Commission. Columnists Evans and Novak reported in their *Exercise of Power* that ever since the end of World War II presidential appointments to the commission were the subject of intense behind-the-scenes lobbying and bitter ideological struggles. The majority that controlled the five-member commission throughout the Eisenhower Administration was pro-industry, enough so to postpone carrying out the Supreme Court's *Phillips Petroleum* decision of 1954, which authorized federal regulation of natural gas prices. In his first year in office, President Kennedy radically changed the complexion of the commission with nominations giving it a 3-to-2 majority in favor of the consumer. One member of that majority was Ross, a peppery Yankee lawyer recommended to Kennedy by Senator George Aiken, the influential and sardonic Vermont Republican who had battled the utilities all his public career.

Industry lobbyists were almost successful in persuading President Johnson not to reappoint Kennedy protégé Ross. "But a vigorous counterlobby on Ross's behalf was started by Senator Aiken, who enlisted the liberals in Congress and the press." The reappointment eventually came through and Charlie Ross served until 1968 on the Federal Power Commission plus nineteen years on the International Joint Commission, which dealt with disputes between the United States and Canada.

This horseman's career was significant for helping to introduce an environmental ethic into federal decision making. The International Joint Commission was a leader in recognizing the importance of transnational pollution. At the Federal Power Commission, Commissioner Ross participated in the famous Storm King case where his dissent led to an appellate opinion usually cited as the subsequent legal basis for environmental law. As Commissioner Ross said in his famous dissent, "I do feel the public is entitled to know on the record that no stone has been left unturned. . . . A regulatory commission can insure [*sic*] continuing confidence in its decisions only when it has used its staff and its own expertise in [a] manner not possible for the uninformed and poorly financed public."

The idea of public service may be about as unfashionable with young people, looking for the big bucks, as a horse and buggy would be to a teenage hotrodder. But I am confident that the national pendulum will swing back toward the tradition of disinterested service exemplified by Charlie Ross and his parents.

P art of the tradition of our family was that they were among the largest, most respected breeders of horses in the late 1800s. So horses were part of my heritage.

My real heroes were my parents. They conveyed to me and

instilled in me a sense of service to the public. In the sense that a person who has some advantages should help his fellow human beings.

My father was a country doctor in Middlebury, Vermont. During the twenties, the end of one transportation era, he had two automobiles. But he couldn't depend on them in the mud season or in a snowstorm. So he had horses. I can remember making calls with him throughout the country before I was in grade school. In a sleigh in the wintertime and in a buggy in the mud season. He enjoyed horses.

My father died when I was nine years of age. He was a very dominant man. Highly respected. People were highly dependent upon him as a country doctor, particularly the people in the outlying districts. People who normally would not get served unless somebody had the willingness and desire to serve them.

My mother also was a very unique person. She was an early graduate of the University of Vermont. She was a Phi Beta Kappa math major back at the turn of the century.

Both my folks were extremely interested in missionary activities and in serving the people. They were the Teddy Roosevelt people. They didn't follow the general line. My father went to Georgia as a medical missionary. Before he died, he was planning to go to China as a medical missionary.

My grandfather on my mother's side had been in horses since about 1850. And his father and grandfather had had one of the largest orchards in New England in Charlotte, Vermont. From about 1850 right through until about 1915, they raised and trained horses as a sideline. They were trying to cross Hambletonian, Messenger, and a number of other extremely well-known thoroughbred stallions to an offspring of Justin Morgan, Ethan Allen 50.

The Morgan horse is so inextricably tied to the life of every Vermonter that it is almost impossible to overlook its role. Moreover, in my case, my mother's family, aside from being farmers and orchardists, were also engaged in the raising and training of horses for more than seventy-five years. The strength, the beauty, and the gentleness of the Morgan horse is an inspiration to every real Vermonter.

Justin Morgan is believed to have been a cross between a thoroughbred and an Arabian. Justin Morgan was actually the name of the man who bought Figure—the horse's original name—as an exchange for a debt. He was a music master; today, in many hymnals, you'll find old-time New England hymns by Justin Morgan.

He brought his young colt back to Vermont and the colt became famous because he was so prepotent. He was able to transmit his

Charles Ross

characteristics to his offspring. In those days the horse was often known by its master; it wasn't very long before "Justin Morgan's horse" became Justin Morgan. He had several very, very famous sons who were bred extensively in the early 1800s. Those sons in turn bred further sons. In each case the dominant characteristics of Justin Morgan came through. The offspring were very, very valuable in Vermont because they were useful for fieldwork, for saddle riding, and as driving horses.

As it turned out, one of Justin Morgan's descendants, Ethan Allen 50, was the fastest racehorse pulling a cart in the United States. He was raised in the Champlain Valley and stood at stud throughout the area. My mother's family had a granddaughter by Ethan Allen 50, which was one of the key founders of a cross they achieved. That cross founded the standard bred horse, which is the horse you see in the sulky races.

In my opinion, the most honorable and satisfying career a person can have is to be a public servant. There are many people who for one reason or another cannot adequately represent or defend their interests in today's complex society. It is a most satisfying experience to serve those who are unable to protect their interests and to instill in everyone a sense of security that the common good is the ultimate goal of society. My parents, more by deeds than by words, were constantly seeking to assist the less fortunate. That is what public service is all about.

By far the greatest struggle in my public career involved securing reappointment by President Johnson to the Federal Power Commission over his intention to replace me. From almost the time of President Kennedy's assassination in November 1963 until March 1965, it was doubtful whether I could survive as a commissioner, despite overwhelming support from many prominent U.S.

senators and widespread editorial endorsements from most major newspapers and many periodicals. That encouraged me to stand firm and to continue to do and say what I thought to be right. But for a short period of time, I wasn't sure whether I could resist the pressure of the president to cave in. I needed the help of my family and most particularly my wife Charlotte, as well as the general encouragement of the public. And the words of support from Senator Aiken, Governor Hoff, and James Oakes (now Second Circuit Court of Appeals judge). When things were darkest, I was encouraged to take a few days off in June 1964 and come to Vermont. I spent those days on Lake Champlain. It wasn't long before I was able to put everything into perspective.

My father was first and foremost a patriot who left his wife and family at an advanced age to volunteer for medical duty overseas in World War I. To question my president was not something to do lightly. Being a history major in college myself, I fully understood the role of the president, but I also had been taught to stand up for what I believed to be right.

With the help of others, I was ultimately reappointed. Much to my surprise, there were no harsh feelings on the part of President Johnson, despite his earlier strong language about the issue.

From that time on, I became more convinced than ever of the importance of standing up for what you believe to be right and of the overwhelming necessity of support and encouragement from your friends and family. I was fortunate to have the strong role models of my father and mother.

Because of my parents, I felt very strongly throughout my career that the environment, which I had enjoyed with them and with other Vermonters, had to be protected. I had hiked the Long Trail, fished the brooks of the Green Mountains and the waters of Lake Champlain, built a log cabin with my brother, cooked out over open fires, and hiked through the forests and fields of rural Vermont.

My father died when I was nine but he taught me the love of the outdoors. My mother carried on when left alone with a young and insatiably curious family. Though she was bedridden during the last four years of her life — she died when I was seventeen — she was determined that we should make a contribution to society and leave it in better condition than we found it.

My parents had faith that they could make an impact on society and I feel the same way. When you see the good that can be accomplished if you have the right attitude, it is awful hard to become cynical.

Discouraged, at times, yes. Cynical, no.

Bernie Sanders

SOCIALIST MAYOR

Burlington, Vermont
Born: 1941

➤➤➤➤➤➤➤➤➤➤➤➤➤➤➤ ⊗ ◄◄◄◄◄◄◄◄◄◄◄◄◄◄◄◄

BERNIE SANDERS IS AN ANOMALY in Vermont politics. Make that *national* politics: His victories as a Socialist mayoral candidate have brought him nationwide attention. He is the rare politician who focuses on issues, not image. He is also the sort of outsider who not long ago would never have gotten to first base in Vermont.

In fact, the Brooklyn, New York native waged several unsuccessful campaigns before reaching the mayor's office of Vermont's largest city. At first his combative style, socialist policies, and Brooklyn accent made his victory seem like a fluke. His initial term corrected that impression with impressive gains for the city in practical matters like street repair, landfill abatement, sewer modernization, and property tax relief. In 1985 he won a seven-way reelection race with 55 percent of the vote.

His chief hero was Eugene V. Debs (1855–1926), Socialist party leader and five-time presidential candidate. Debs did prison time for espousing his pro-peace, anti-establishment views. So did another of Sanders' heroes, Martin Luther King, Jr. Such heroes and views may be out of fashion in America in the eighties, but in the north country, populism is as indigenous as the Green Mountain Boys.

Seventh-generation Vermonter and former state senator Graham Newell of St. Johnsbury recently paid a high compliment to Burlington's feisty mayor. "Bernie Sanders," he said, "is becoming a good Vermonter because he's so damn independent."

On the wall over there is a picture of Eugene Debs. That record cover is an album I produced six or seven years ago on the life of Eugene Debs. He ran for president five times and is to me one of the important heroes of American history.

Probably the vast majority of school kids have never head of him.

What Debs believed then reads quite as well today as when he wrote it. He was an extraordinarily brave man who went to jail a number of times fighting for peace or for the rights of workers. He spoke his mind and told the truth. He said there's something very wrong about the fact that we live in a society where wealth and power are controlled by a few and where workers have to scratch to stay alive.

So Debs is one of my important heroes. My political philosophy is very close to his. The difference is that, for better or for worse, I was elected and he wasn't.

When you get elected you have to change your strategies a little bit and do the best you can. Debs on the outside was more able to articulate ideas that eventually became acceptable. And I have to implement policy today. But ultimately the vision Debs had for America and the world is very close to what mine is.

Debs ended up going to jail in opposition to World War I. During that time, the Socialist party was attacked vigorously by the federal government because it was gaining influence. When World War I broke out, the left wing of the Socialist party felt that it was a war between imperialist factions of the world and that it didn't make any sense for American workers to go out and get killed in it. Which I think was the right position. The American government didn't think too highly of that and smashed many Socialist party offices and arrested and deported many people. Debs gave a speech in which he supported the rights of workers not to enlist in the Army. He ended up in jail.

What Debs was talking about was nothing more than justice. Here in the city of Burlington in the last year we have fought with the Federal Aviation Administration, the restaurant owners, the Chamber of Commerce, the private utilities, the phone company, and with big businesses all over the place. They're spending hundreds and hundreds of thousands of dollars fighting various initiatives we are developing, all of which try to give a break to the average person. That's what justice is about.

Being a mayor is not a very sexy job. Very often you're dealing with nuts-and-bolts type things. Also, our political organizations and government structures make it very hard to do the things you want to do. Cities have very little power.

Today, for example, the city won a major victory in our right to develop an excavation fee that will charge utilities for digging up city streets. Previously that never existed. No Vermont city or town had ever developed it. It is a breakthrough in Vermont history.

It's not all that significant, but it took us months and months and months. The utilities spent hundreds of thousands of dollars

Bernie Sanders

fighting us. This gets back to the question of heroes. When you're up against the system, it is very hard to be heroic because your options are usually the lesser of two evils. In this case the excavation fee is nothing more than an attempt to raise revenue with which to fix deteriorating streets and sidewalks. OK? Historically the streets were dug up by private utilities; they never paid us a nickel. Now they are going to pay us. It's not any great or terribly progressive tax. It has taken us a year to make this fight; the fight will continue. Constantly there are lies about our intentions.

The point is that as mayor you don't *win*. It's not like invading Grenada and coming out the victor. Every day there's another problem and every day you've got to move along with it.

What I'm trying to do is to balance a long term vision of what this country can be with being the best possible mayor right now. It's quite a juggling act.

I think my vision is of a radically different type of society. The society we live in is a cruel, unfair society. We have a handful of individuals and corporations and banks who make the major decisions. We have people sitting home watching crap put on television by large corporations attempting to lie or distort. We have an educational system throughout the country that is inadequate and higher education that is less and less open to working-class people. A medical profession that is more concerned about private profit than the welfare of people. I can go on and on. It is not a system that develops human potential. Also, it's a system that may very well get us into nuclear war.

Primarily because of the nature of the media, politicians do not discuss issues. Anything that I say could be taken out of context and blown up. Therefore politicians by necessity become very conservative, as I have. I often read from prepared remarks. You're writing a book, and a book is one thing, but at my press conference here this afternoon I read from a prepared statement. I'm very careful about what I say because the media love sensationalism. If you make one silly statement or mistake, it's something you live for your entire life. So you become very cautious about that.

The advantage I have is that in a small city like Burlington, after four years the people get to know you. Either they trust you or they don't trust you. We are now engaged in an extremely bitter campaign where one of my opponents is just making one false statement after another. If half the people end up believing him, I will lose. I don't think they will. They know me well enough not to believe him. We're a *small* city and I'm gonna knock on a lot of doors. I know thousands of people personally.

It's hard to destroy somebody's character—which is the nature of politics—if people know him personally. You have to have personal contact to get your message out.

I think the whole question of heroes is very interesting. I think a hero is somebody people respect because he or she is doing something brave or unusual. Often standing up to the powers that be. Given the nature of our system, and especially the media, it is very unlikely that you can have for a sustained period a hero who is standing up to the special interests. One way or another, he's going to get knocked down.

For instance, a guy like Martin Luther King, Jr., who today is regarded as a great hero, was maligned in the last few years of his life. He was not a hero. People have forgotten that. He was having a difficult time getting into the newspapers. He had lost the glow. It was OK for King to be a leader in the Civil Rights movement and to take on segregation. That the System approved of. But when he began speaking out about the war in Vietnam or when he began speaking out on the need for black and white workers to come together for economic justice, he was no longer a hero.

I think that after you do away with phraseology like socialism and conservatism what you find out is whether people are entitled to earn a decent living and get a fair shake from government and whether the corporations that have wealth and power are obliged to pay their fair share of taxes. These are not very complicated issues.

Socialism is an international philosophy, but I think that once you start talking about issues and reality rather than terminology, what we say makes a good deal of sense to people in Vermont.

Alfred E. Smith

GADFLY

Lyndonville, Vermont
Born: 1917

THE VILLAGE ATHEIST HAS all but disappeared from Vermont towns, along with creameries and snow rollers. Alfred E. Smith endures in this role like an antique steam train shuttling summer tourists. Except that this public meeting gadfly is a year-round institution.

With the almost complete secularization of society, atheism is no longer the outré subject of passionate debate it was in the time of Alfred's anticlerical heroes, Thomas Paine (1737–1809) and Robert Green Ingersoll (1833–1899). After all, who can care about godlessness when there is the Game to watch, the lawn to mow, and the new gadgets to master?

Despite Smith's strenuous proselytizing, I was not ready to believe that either Thomas Paine or Robert Green Ingersoll was America's greatest hero. But I was fascinated by Alfred's devotion. He does not approach these men with the dispassionate curiosity of a scholar but with the fervor of a true believer. That same enthusiasm enlivens all his public tussles. He only half-jokingly said of the doctor who opposed him recently in a gun control debate, "We know this doctor is wrong because he's a flatlander."

But Lyndonville's gadfly does not lack in ways to needle his neighbors. Let's take the subject of snow removal as an example. Probably nothing excites more people more quickly in Vermont than the subject of winter roads. And Alfred E. Smith, who is not a traveler, wants to stop the town from spreading salt and gravel.

Although Alfred know that many people think he is a crank, it doesn't faze him a bit. In fact, he relishes the notoriety.

He *is* very quotable and often appears in newspaper accounts of public meeting with statements like, "Some Vermonters used to be frugal, but there's almost none of those left." Or, "If this nuclear arms freeze should be effected, you had better begin to learn the Russian language — which *I* have no intention of doing." Or, "There are not many real Vermonters left. The old-timers have died off and the flatlanders have moved in and we're going the way of modernization." And, "I know from past history that the Democrats are always wrong and the Republicans are usually wrong."

A few years ago, three masked men broke into his house and beat him severely, breaking his jaw. When I heard about it, I immediately assumed that they were ideological foes, though in retrospect they were more likely inspired by rumors that the ever-frugal Alfred was hoarding his money. (It's a mystery why burglars would think they'd find anything inside Alfred's rundown, wood frame house. Outside he has made significant savings on house paint over the last many decades. "If you don't spend a dime," he says, "you save two cents in interest.")

This frugal small operator worked in sawmills, in a plastics factory, and moving and mixing grain at the Ralston Purina plant. To him his lack of formal education is a plus because "the school system doesn't teach much of value."

In a Vermont town like Lyndonville, opportunities abound for a determined gadfly at school board meetings (the "poorest, most boring outfit you can imagine") and biweekly selectmen's and town trustees' meetings. Alfred E. Smith attends meetings as regularly as milking time. (That's him standing in the photo, addressing the trustees.) Best of all is the annual town meeting, "where" he states, "the teachers and their relatives come out to vote for the continuation of the school system."

You might think that I did not like Alfred E. Smith. In fact, he himself hinted as much several times. He was wrong: I *do* appreciate him and I hope you will, too. You do not have to agree with him to appreciate his good points. Like the sense of humor he showed last January when he reminded me that Vermont has nine months of winter and three months of poor sledding. And like his famous persistence.

And he may, after all, succeed eventually with his antisalt campaign.

The thing to remember is that public meetings do deserve our attention. The danger in our democracy is that individuals will not take responsibility for the public's business. Alfred E. Smith, whatever his quirks, is always ready to participate. Often he is the only one. I think his friend Bill Cummings summed it up best when he said, "Sometimes Alfred embarrasses the people who introduce these harebrained schemes enough that they withdraw their proposals and let them die off behind the barn somewhere."

I was enough of an age so that I was aware of the bad situation during the Depression. That's why I'm all for being very frugal, not living way beyond our means, and paying for things as we go.

I would not want the people here to experience a Depression. Of course, *we* got along good during the Depression. But most people didn't. We had six cows here. And my father worked out. He was a great worker and then some. He was doing a man's job when he was about eleven years old. And he seemed to like to work. He wasn't too great for education, but he used his head a little. And he saved money. Here in the town, one woman used to say that my father had an unusual ability. He could earn fifty cents and save seventy-five cents of it.

I would like no more salt and sand to be used on the roads. The people here are quite unreasonable. They think we can have summer roads in winter. In order to do that, you've got to use salt and sand, which is very expensive.

Originally in this area the people did nothing about the roads in winter. The horses just waded through and packed it down some. Later they used to roll the roads with a roller made of wood, probably ten or twelve feet wide and five or six feet in diameter with a seat on top for the driver of the roller's team of horses. So that's the way they got over the roads in winter; they packed em down.

Nineteen hundred and thirty-three was about the last year they rolled the roads here in the town. Thereafter they began to plow them.

The ruts used to be awful deep when they were just plowing the roads and not using salt. Here on Main Street in the Ville there would be several sets of tire tracks. Sometimes the front wheels and the rear wheels would be in separate sets of ruts. If you wanted

Alfred E. Smith (standing)

to get out of your ruts to turn onto a side street and you couldn't, you stopped your car, took out your axe, and notched the ruts so that the wheels would come into this notch. Then you could turn to the right or left, whichever you needed to do. Oh, that was a lot of work.

People wanted better roads than that. They put on a lot of salt so that they could have practically bare pavement during winter, which is very costly. But everybody's got to drive at summer speeds. These people just do not realize that we have winter here.

I'm for plowing the roads but not for putting on salt. The cost of salt has gone up a lot; I think it's about thirty dollars a ton now. The town garage is right next door to me and they bring in many, many long trailer loads of salt every year. That costs money.

To prevent the ruts from getting deep, I'd use a road machine to scrape the ice off. That is, lower the depth of the ice so it would be pretty good going. Years ago people put on chains and they got along good.

When the cost of salt was brought up recently, one of the selectmen said he'd like to reduce the use of salt. But if you reduce the use of salt, then a lot of people complain. And if you use the salt, then other people complain because of the damage the salt does.

The selectmen are surely in the middle and surrounded. Mostly by me. [*Laughter.*]

Thomas Paine and Robert Green Ingersoll were not afraid to put their thoughts into good English. I like their reasoning, which is far better than most people's. They were outstanding at their times. Thomas Paine was the number one citizen of this country and Robert Green Ingersoll is probably the second greatest individual this country ever had. His nomination of Blaine at the Republican national convention in 1876 was one of the outstanding speeches ever made in the English language.

Ingersoll grew up in a religious family. His father was a minister who traveled quite a bit here and there. When Ingersoll began to study the Bible and the background of it, he realized that Thomas Paine knew what he was talking about. And that Thomas Paine had hardly scratched the surface of what the Bible means. It just goes to show that these people were altogether different than the general run of people. They were independent thinkers.

Few people know who Ingersoll was. You see, the churches in the past have run the government. The pulpit runs the schoolhouses and has for years. But that's beginning to change.

A few years after my father died, there came the issue of building a new school for the town, to replace the one-room schools where kids could walk to school with expensive busing. I have no kids, not only here but overseas, too. [*Laughter.*] But I first became involved in town affairs when they started to plan for the new school. Because when certain groups try to put something over on you, that is, their brainy idea which is very expensive and we can't afford . . .

I never know what I'm going to do at a meeting. I may read a condemnation letter for the school board.

Whether it's local or state or federal, I am much opposed to our officials because they do not do right and they do not even have the right ideas. Even two days ago at the zoning board the officials did awfully wrong. Just recently because of finding pollution in our water from the dump all of the local and state officials want to clean up the dump. Which is absolutely impossible because this liquid has gone down through the ground for years and spread out. You can't remove those millions of cubic yards and haul them many, many miles.

I told two state men a week ago that they had no morality. If the stuff isn't good enough for us, it's not good enough for anybody else. We shouldn't wish our trouble on some other state. That's not right. We've got it here; we've got to live with it.

I used to go regularly to the school board meetings but they are long and drawn out and they accomplish nothing. You would think that in the school board meetings there would be some really intelligent stuff going on, but they're the poorest, most boring outfit you can imagine. And I've told em so.

I'm very careful what I want because I don't want to have to pay for the things. The other people want everything imaginable, in particular when they can get somebody else to pay their part.

Preston "Jack" Smith

SNOWPLOW DRIVER

Wheelock, Vermont

➤➤➤➤➤➤➤➤➤➤➤➤➤➤➤➤ ⊛ ◄◄◄◄◄◄◄◄◄◄◄◄◄◄◄◄◄◄◄◄◄

FOR YEAR ROUND RESIDENTS, VERMONT MEANS snow and lots of it. The white stuff starts falling sometime before memories of summer have cooled and it barely melts off in time for mud season. Some years may be whiter than others, but drivers inevitably face long months of snow, ice, slush, and every heart skip of wintery hazard. I have heard it said that anyone who regularly gets behind the wheel will also get into the ditch at least once during a Vermont winter.

So snow removal excites strong passions. But have you ever wondered how the snowplow driver sees it? The interesting thing about Wheelock road commissioner Jack Smith is that he is such an even–tempered fellow. Storms come and go. Drivers smash into his big rig. He faces it all with an equanimity astonishing to the person uptight about a few snowflakes or a little glare ice.

But don't be deceived by that calm figure up there in the big cab. Jack Smith *has* been around road work a long time; his father was once Sheffield's road commissioner and was the teamster featured in Dean McDowell's horse pulling dream. Jack learned his heavy equipment skills from a real master out in Colorado, where Jack and his family once foolishly settled. Despite all that experience, one kind of weather can be as hard on Jack Smith as on any Sunday driver.

What he really fears is a midwinter *rain*. A nasty squall or a good old-fashioned gullywasher can make ice and snow as slick as deer guts on a doorknob. That's when a man, even a snowplow man, can begin to feel his age. "I don't go for rain at this time of year," he says. "Sliding around puts gray hairs on my head. You take a piece of equipment about the size of our truck and put, oh, seven, eight yards of sand on it and you get it sliding backward down a hill, that'll age you in a hurry!"

I was born in the town of Sheffield and lived here all my life, except that time I put in the service and the year I was in Colorado. I went to work for a construction outfit out there. Jim Fitzhugh was a blade operator and he taught me more about how to run a grader and about what it could do and wouldn't do than I learned in all my time in the service. The Army had some good instructors, but I guess it was just Jim's easy way of explaining things while we were doing them. He and I worked together the better part of six months. He was a typical Westerner. Easygoing. You know: If we don't get it today, we'll get it tomorrow. Nothing seemed to upset him.

Jim was about fifty-seven years old when I was out there. A charming personality. He was what I'd call a super nice guy. If you asked him a question, he went beyond answering it so that you would understand the whole area of the answer.

Vermonters are easygoing, I guess, but I found that there's a considerable difference between our way of life and that out West. Ours is . . . We're not so apt to come right out and say, "We're here to do this or we're here to do that." But if a person gets in trouble, they don't have to look too far; the help is there. I guess I'd have to say that we just don't brag on it.

We were gone about a year. We came back to Vermont because we were homesick. [*Laughter.*] I was. My wife was. My children were. So we decided to move back.

I've been road commissioner about seven years. It is and it isn't a hard job. It's tedious work sometimes. But everything runs together. I maintain the roads during the summertime and also do the plowing and sanding during the wintertime. So I have a good idea of how the roads lay. That's an absolute must. If you don't know where the roads are and what they are, you can put a truck in the ditch so easy that it's pathetic. Especially this time of year, with our snowbanks the way they are. We run right on the edge of the ditch, so if we get over just a little bit, we're off the road and stuck.

Then you have to get something to get you out.

I've been stuck. I maintain that if you don't get stuck, you're not getting your road out far enough.

With the amount of traffic on the road today, you have to be extremely careful with that size equipment. I've been run into three times. Too much speed in all instances. The drivers weren't paying attention. I had one lady who slid clear through an intersection and hit us in the rear. And one who came sliding around a corner and hit me, though I put my rig clear off the road to try to get away

Preston "Jack" Smith

from her. It didn't do too much damage to mine, but it did a number on hers.

With the exception of the International Scout that hit me, the other two cars were pretty well totaled. You don't move one of these trucks in a hurry. You can't get it out of the way the same as you can a small automobile. The best you can do is to get where they ain't gonna hit you too bad.

People drive a lot faster than they should, especially on the back roads. The back roads aren't as wide as maybe they should be, even during the summer. People have a tendency to leave late and drive fast. If I had just one winter driving tip, I would say slow down. On some hills you do have to kick it along in order to get over the top, but there again, if you're running a good set of snow tires, too much speed is just as bad as not enough. You've got to let the weight of the vehicle carry it along.

In the past few years, it seems to me that our winter weather has changed drastically. When I was growing up, the cold came in the latter part of October. We got a thaw in January. Then in March the spring came and the snow went. But lately it seems that we get wet, rainy weather much later into the year. Along in November and even into December. It's odd to me that it can rain when it's 26 degrees, but it does.

I have seen it when the Stannard Mountain Road over in South Wheelock was all glare ice down below, yet up on top it was bare right down to the dirt because of the warm air that set up high.

If we get a bad snowfall, meaning if we get anywhere from six to eight inches on up, then I put both machines on the road. My truck and the grader, too. And whip it out as fast as we can. Otherwise, both of us go on the truck because we like to keep two people together. It makes everything a lot easier. If you get into a bind, you'll have help.

We start at six o'clock in the morning now, but if we got a bad snowstorm, we'd probably start at four.

Right around six o'clock there's a time when everything whites out. Everything blends together. Quite often the guy that's riding shotgun can tell you that you're crowding the bank or that you're beginning to pull back into the middle of the road and you can't see it yourself.

By the time I've plowed from the church at the Four Corners over Stannard Mountain and back, it has snowed two-and-a-half to three inches. We have thirty miles of road to plow. By the time we get done plowing, we've done over a hundred miles because we have to make four passes over each part. Two trips over and two back.

I think the worst storm we had was in December. It was a combination of snow and ice. We were four hours cutting our way over the top of Stannard Mountain because the ice took down maple trees. It just dropped those trees right into the road. We had to stop and cut them with a chainsaw and move the brush and stuff out of the way. It took four hours to go three miles.

This February it snowed about thirteen days. But no large accumulation. It's all powdery like feathers; you can whistle right along fifteen, twenty-five miles an hour and blow it off the road.

When you get into a snowstorm like the last big one we had last year, where we were supposed to pick up three to five inches and we got thirty, then you can't blow it off the road. You've got to push it back. Then push it back again. If you get four or five inches of wet snow, you can handle it real good. But once you start getting upwards of a foot, then you've got quite a little problem to get it shoved back and hammered into place.

It you get a large amount of snow, it'll push your whole truck and plow sideways because of the way the plow is angled. So you have to keep backing up and hitting it. About the only rig you can open up a road with then is a V-plow and we don't have one of those.

But we do all right.

It's all in getting used to the work. Just like getting used to driving a car or a pick-up truck. That thirteen-foot snowplow looks monstrous coming head-on at somebody, but sitting behind it you don't notice.

I enjoy my work. Every now and then there's some oddball thing. I was grading up on Stannard one day and had my road signs out and there I was crossways in the road turning around. This car came down at about fifty-five miles an hour. I had a big pile of dirt in the middle of the road and they hit that. Needless to say, they weren't very happy. I thought it was kinda comical myself.

Darwin Everett "Rocky" Stone

DOWSER

Sutton, Vermont
Born: 1925

✦>✦>✦>✦>✦>✦>✦>✦>✦>✦> ⊗ ✦<✦<✦<✦<✦<✦<✦<✦<✦<✦<✦

ROCKY STONE IS A RETIRED industrial arts teacher from Connecticut. A few years ago he and his wife Alice moved to Hardscrabble Mountain beyond Sutton to build a log cabin. Up on their dry ridge the urgent question of water needed an immediate solution.

Rocky would be the last person to claim that he understands dowsing, but he does live in an area so attuned to that subject that it hosts an annual dowsing convention. Of the local experts, the professor emeritus was the late Fay Young.

I guess a sensible man should reserve judgment about something like dowsing, even if he *has* felt the Power through his own hands.

It was back in 1969. The wife and I decided that we would build a log cabin up here in the Northeast Kingdom. And, of course, grandfather taught me a long time ago when we were rammin around in the woods that the first thing you do when you set up any kind of permanent camp is to make darned sure that you've got a good water supply. Before I invested too much time or effort in clearing the land or starting a cabin, I decided that I'd better find out for sure whether or not we had water.

There was a black family lived up on top of the mountain by the name of Wood. There was Ed and Josephine Wood and they had a whole passel of kids up there they'd raised and had sent some of em to college. He was an itinerant carpenter and handyman and never took anything from anybody for nothing. He always earned it. Anyway, I went to see old Woody and Woody said, "Well, I don't know whether there's water there or not, but we can find out."

I said, "How's that?"

"Well, maybe you have the Power. Maybe you can dowse it."

I said, "C'mon, Woody. I don't understand that stuff or even believe in it."

He said, "Josephine can do it, but I can't."

I said, "Well, all right. Ain't nobody around to see me, so I guess I can get away with it."

He cut a forked branch off an apple bush, trimmed it up, and showed me how to hold it. He said, "Walk out through there."

I felt very foolish, but I walked over there holding the stick as I was instructed. Feeling for sure that nothing was gonna happen. I walked along until pretty soon the hair on the back of my neck kinda tingled a little bit and the next thing I knew that stick went down. I was holding it so tight that it practically took the bark off the part I was holding. You could hear it squeak. I swore to myself, Well, I must have done something to do that. 'Cause I couldn't see how it had happened.

Woody saw it and he said, "All right, let go of the stick and walk up beyond there and come back toward me and do the same thing."

And I did and, lo and behold, the stick went down again.

Altogether we found what seemed like five streams coming in to one central point. Woody thought we had found the best place for a well. But I wasn't sure about it at all.

One thing he did kinda convinced me, though. He said, "As I told you, I can't do it. But it's dipped very strongly for you, especially here in this central spot. Let me show you." He took the stick and held it just the way I had. He walked right over that spot and the stick didn't even quiver. He said, "Put your hand up on the back of my neck and with the other hand take hold of one branch of the stick." I put my hand up on his neck and I reach out and touched that stick and that stick whipped right down. I'll tell ya, I felt just a little bit peculiar about the whole thing.

But I still wasn't convinced.

There was another fella in town that Woody told me about, a man name of Wallace Ingalls who was in the business of putting in wells. And he dowsed.

I got ahold of Wallace. After half-a-dozen or so phone calls and promises that he'd be up and he'd be up, well, finally he showed up. I didn't say anything to him about what I had found. I just said, "I want to get a well in and I want to have it up in this area above me."

When he went up there, I didn't go with him at all. Pretty soon he came back down. He said, "As near as I can tell, you've got five springs all coming into a central point."

I said, "Is that right?" feeling a little funny about it.

He said, "Yup."

I asked when he thought he could put in a well. Trying to get Wallace Ingalls to come out was one of those difficult things up here where people are always as they say, "straight out." They get around to you when they can; they're going straight out all the time without any pauses.

I heard about another man who Woody said was the professor emeritus of the dowsing fraternity. A man by the name of Fay Young. F. A. Y.—those were his initials. I kept calling and leaving messages for him to call back. Of course, he never did. Finally I met someone in the village who knew that he was working in East Burke putting in a well. I drove over there and followed the sound of a backhoe. The noise seemed to be coming closer. And pretty soon through the brush here comes Mr. Young. I thought for a minute he wasn't going to stop, but he did.

I said, "Hello, are you Mr. Young?"

He said, "Yeah."

I said, "Well, I'm Rocky Stone and I'm building a place over in Sutton and I'd like to see about getting a well in."

"Is that a fact?" he said.

I went on asking him about when he could come over and he wouldn't give me a definite answer. He kept hedging around about it, which is typical. So finally I said, "Well, look Mr. Young, I hate to keep insisting, but I'd like to know when I can expect you to come over."

"Now just a damn minute," he said. "See this cap?" He had on a baseball cap. "That covers the entire family. That's all the responsibility I got is what's under that cap and I work when I've a mind to."

I said, "OK," figuring that I'd blown the whole deal right there.

He said, "Another thing. I wish you'd quit calling me Mr. Young. My name's Fay. *F, A, Y.* Get it?"

I said, "OK, Mr. Fay."

He said, "That's better."

I still tried to get an answer out of him, and he finally said, "Look, if I told you I was going to be there Thursday at nine o'clock, I'd be obliged to be there. So I'm not gonna tell ya."

That night I went home and the wife asked me if I had gotten him to come. I said, "I don't know but I've got a hunch he'll be here Thursday."

Sure enough, Thursday morning about nine o'clock I hear the chug-chug of his old backhoe coming up the road. And there he was, a rangy fella, probably six foot plus, a typical Vermont type.

He looked like he was in his sixties but he was well up in his seventies then. He said, "This machine's a '56 and I'm seventy six; does that tell ya anything?" Well, it didn't tell me anything except that he was older than the machine.

I didn't say anything to him about what Ingalls or I had found. He went up there and dowsed the area while I stayed down below.

Pretty soon he came back and said, "You have five streams up there that seem to be going into one central point and that's where you ought to put your well."

I laughed and said, "OK, I guess maybe it is."

While he was there, we had some people visiting from down country. They were doubting Thomases. They had just gotten out of college and were well-educated and didn't believe in this old folklore.

So he said, "I'll tell you what I'll do. I'll take a dollar bill out of my pocket and while I'm out of the room you select somebody to put it in their pocket."

He did that and left the room. We gave the dollar bill to this young fella who was one of the biggest doubting Thomases in the bunch. Fay came back with his stick and put a dollar bill into the stick. He started walking around the people in the room and stopped right in front of this young fella. That stick went right down just like that. And he says, "You've got my dollar bill; I wish you'd give it to me."

He said, "If that's not proof enough for ya, take this dime out in that tall grass and drop it anywhere and I'll go out and find it."

So I did. I took a dime out there and put it down and made sure it wasn't glimmering or anything.

I'm a son-of-a-gun if he didn't come out and put a dime in the end of that darned stick. He walked back and forth, back and forth, and finally that stick dipped and he reached down and picked up the dime.

I'm not saying that it works and I'm not saying that it doesn't work. There are people that'll swear by dowsing. I'm reserving judgment until I'm in a better position to make a call on it. That's where my well is today and we've always had good water.

Mr. Young, excuse me, Fay, was quite a gentleman. One of a vanishing breed. He's since passed away. Of course, I don't know what did it. He didn't last long after he eloped when he was about ninety. He just went off and when he showed up maybe a month later he was married. Maybe that did him in, but if it did, I suppose he died happy.

John Tuccillo
and Clyde Hunter

VIOLINMAKERS

Lyndonville, Vermont

➤➤➤➤➤➤➤➤➤➤➤➤➤➤➤ ✳ ◄◄◄◄◄◄◄◄◄◄◄◄◄◄◄◄◄

BOTH MEN ARE STUBBORN. And both take their violin-making as seriously as ever did Stradivarius and *his* teacher Amati centuries earlier. John Tuccillo and Clyde Hunter began a few years ago as student and mentor but they have progressed to being friendly rivals.

Clyde Hunter was born on the second day of this century and he may well see the twenty-first century, because, as he says, music has kept him young. A Vermont farmer of the old school, he became an instrument-maker through a trade for a broken-down fiddle. John Tuccillo came to it through a music-loving Italian immigrant family in Mechanicville, New York.

Clyde's music tends toward the play-by-ear fiddle tunes prevalent at the turn-of-the-century; John's taste favors thirties and forties hits like "The Downtown Strutters Ball." Each tries to learn from the other, but old habits and old age slow their efforts.

Clyde Hunter put in thirty-four years with Vermont Tap and Die in Lyndonville. John Tuccillo is a former milk processor who now, in retirement, does plumbing and electrical work. Seeing them having fun arguing and playing their homemade instruments together was a great treat. As child of the century Clyde Hunter said, "I don't profess to play very good, but I get a lot of fun out of it."

In 1932 Clyde made his first violin, an unadorned model with a simple maple back. It had more of a homemade look than his newer ones, perhaps because he had no electrical tools to use a half century ago. The later ones are patterned less on Stradivarius and are crafted more in the Amati style.

Clyde scrapes hesitantly through an old fiddle tune, followed by John fluently playing Italian favorites like "Return to Sorrento" on a 1982 spruce and bird's eye maple instrument. He apologizes: His fingers are not responding well today because he has been repairing boilers.

Clyde Hunter leaves me with an irresistible Vermont-flavored insight into violin-making. "You have to thin the violin wood down to such proportions that it vibrates," he says. "Making a violin is not like making a kitchen cupboard."

JOHN TUCCILLO

Every night I had to play the violin for my cousin who had just come from Italy. He was my mother's cousin and he could play anything. Right away my mother figured I should play violin. He could play trumpet, accordian, guitar, mandolin, flute, piano. So he taught a couple of the fellas his age—he was about nineteen—and within a year and a half we were playing at a lot of Italian weddings. There was a beer joint, a speakeasy, next to my house—this was before Prohibition—where local fellas could buy a bottle of homebrew or a couple of glasses of wine and listen to the nickelodeon and play cards or pool.

We'd play our instruments there and the older guys would get half drunk; I'd get a bottle of soda out of it. I got so I hated the violin. I was never so happy as when my cousin moved to Columbus, Ohio. That was the end of my lessons.

Oh, I was fond of him all right. But my mother! I wanted to play ball and she wanted me to practice.

Then I didn't touch the violin for forty-five years. I'm almost seventy-three years old now.

After I had been here twenty years, I met Clyde. We played violin together and he kept harping on the subject of my making one. I used to like to work with wood, so one day I decided to shut him up: I made one. Then he wondered how I made it so fast. Actually, it was still in an experimental stage.

As you work on violins, you learn a few tricks. I read some books and that helped a lot. In fact, I learned something today. It used to take me all day to make a violin rib; I made one in five minutes today.

Clyde showed me how to use certain tools. But there really isn't very much anyone can tell you without your doing it yourself and finding out. He looks over my work and he tells me if I'm right or wrong. But we argue all the time about how to make em. He makes em the old-fashioned way; I make em the new way. You're supposed to take your time and do it slow, but I don't have the patience. He has a lot of it.

I'm making violins now just to see if I can keep making em better, because I'm never satisfied. I've made five violins and a viola and I'm still not satisfied with em. I don't know what I'm doing wrong but I'm gonna hit it one of these days.

I'm trying to change him. That's where the student gets smarter than the teacher. I like to prove things to myself. I try it his way and I try it mine. Well, I don't know yet which way to go.

CLYDE HUNTER

My mother was a musician. She never took a music lesson in her life but she could play anything on the piano. "Golden Slippers." Waltzes. She could pick around a little and see what key somebody was playing in and play right along. My father could play the violin. His sister was a music teacher.

When I was about eight years old, I used to have to go get the cows about five at night. While I was gone after the cows, my mother would play the piano. She'd start in before I went. That was about the only time she had. I'd hear it before I went after the cows. It's natural for me to like music.

I was fourteen years old when I went after the cows one night and I got wet. I had a cold, anyway, so my father and mother went down to the barn to do the milking and I stayed home. I got Dad's fiddle out from under the couch and when they came back from the barn I had figured it out and I played "Jingle Bells" for em. That was the first time I learned on Dad's fiddle. I've played ever since.

I was a farmer before we came down to Lyndonville in 1929. My father was always building a house or a barn or a mill for somebody; I did the farm work. He would help me get the crops in after I had plowed and planted them.

We always did everything that came along: carpentry work, masonry work, no matter what it was. I went and built a cupboard for a couple on a farm and they had an old violin. We had a nice one, but I thought I wanted that old one. I took it for building the cupboard. It took me a week to build that cupboard; I did a good job with it.

That violin needed some fixin. It was rough as a plowed field inside, which a lot of em are. I took it all apart, smoothed it up, graduated it, and replaced the baseboard, which had been too light. After I got it fixed, it sounded beautiful. I gave it to my mother.

I had such good luck fixing that one that I decided to make a fiddle. I still have the first one I made in 1932. I used a Stradivarius pattern, but I made it deeper. I had my own ideas; I'm stubborn like John is. He and I can't agree on certain things.

When I retired from the Tap and Die, I wanted to be doing something, so I went looking for wood. I found some maple in North Montpelier that was supposed to go into a table top and I made three fiddlebacks from that. Three fiddles, three violas, and a combination violin and viola.

John has read all the books. I never read any, but I've experimented. A friend from Massachusetts had seen a genuine Stradivarius violin and said that it had a pinkish color inside. Well, that gave me a thought right off that it must have had something inside.

I bought a violin from a fella in East St. Johnsbury that wasn't worth a nickel. It had a mess of gumbo on it. I took that off and took the top off and I graduated that. I painted a coat of light glue, about as thin as light cream, all over the inside. When it dried, I smoothed it off with light sandpaper. You'd never know there was a thing in it but the bare wood.

Well, I've tried to convince John that glue helps a fiddle but he's read the books and the books don't tell him to do that. So he won't do it. That's why he and I differ.

JOHN TUCCILLO: I'm sorry now I didn't play more and take my mother's advice. I think they should teach more music in school because that's something you can use all your life.

CLYDE HUNTER: Music has kept me young. I've enjoyed John's coming to play. [*Clyde haltingly plays the "Shannon Waltz."*] Linseed oil is all I've got on the outside of my fiddle. John's got a filler and violin varnish.

JOHN TUCCILLO: But I don't believe in oil. I'll varnish, but I size it; I don't have it go into the wood.

CLYDE HUNTER: He puts on a filler so it can't go into the wood. But you know, he sounds beautiful with my fiddles. He sounds beautiful with any fiddle. I've been trying to get him to put glue on the inside and boiled linseed oil on the outside, but he won't do it. I think he will eventually.

JOHN TUCCILLO: Never, Clyde! Never.

CLYDE HUNTER: It sure doesn't hurt em any.

JOHN TUCCILLO: Yes, it does!

CLYDE HUNTER: I don't think so!

John Tuccillo (right) and Clyde Hunter

Joseph Tuttle

FARMER

Tunbridge, Vermont

IF OLD-FASHIONED VERMONT FARMING had been easier, the Tuttles of Tunbridge might not have been so long-lived. At least that is the theory of
hard-working, hard-drinking Joseph Tuttle. He has not quite matched his
grandmother Mahala's ninety-three years of age or his maternal grandfather's ninety eight, but I am confident that he will. He has buried two
wives, and remarried a third time in 1980. I found it very appropriate that
he should have such a hold on life because he lives surrounded by Tuttle
history. Every room in his sprawling farmhouse is full of nineteenth-
century photos and mementos.

Joe's paternal grandfather used to be gone two or three weeks while
driving his sheep and turkeys to market in Boston. (That's "driving" as in
sheep drive, not as in automobiles.) The family then lived on Tuttle Hill,
named after Joe's great-grandfather; they moved to their present place in
1872. It had originally been settled in 1774 by Nathaniel Pease; the present
house was built in 1810.

A Civil War diary, metal letter box, and a Currier and Ives rendition of
the battle of Petersburg, Virginia are constant reminders of an uncle who
died tragically in the closing days of the Civil War.

And Joe's maternal grandfather came to Vermont by canoe up the Connecticut River.

Shortly after visiting Joe Tuttle, I was out West where I met a thirty-
year-old Californian who had rejected his father's Boston and Italian background. This déraciné son was "into" various trendy activities; his wife had
just "split for L.A." Between them, they probably did not have a smidgin
of the sense of family tradition that Joe Tuttle felt about every room of
his farmhouse.

Family, land, and continuity are a big part of what makes Vermont special. But pinning down this quality is difficult. Vermont can be an almost

indefinable attitude. Listen for it in the following story about Joe Tuttle's school days.

"When I was a boy going to school, the neighbors brought a boy up here from the Little Wonders Home, a home for poor kids down in Boston.

"Harold was older than I was but we used to walk to school together. He was a nice fella.

"The post office was in the country store and at Christmastime we went in one night to get the mail. There were some fur caps on the counter, and, while the clerk was busy sorting the mail, Harold put his cap in his pocket and grabbed one of those and put it on and walked out.

"Well, when we got up the road a ways he threw his old cap away. 'Joe,' he said, 'don't you wish you could get a cap like that the way I did?'

'Harold, I wasn't brought up that way,' I said.

"My father went down to the store and told the storekeeper about it.

"Well, the next night the boy and I went in there after supper and the storekeeper came along. 'Boy,' he said, 'that's a pretty good hat. Where'd you get it?'

"'Oh,' he said, 'Gramps went to Sears Roebuck and got it.'

"He said, 'You care if I look at it?'

"'No.'

"So the storekeeper took it and looked at it and turned the flap down and there was his tag in there. He said, 'Boy, I guess you took that off the counter here last night.'

"'Yeah,' Harold said.

"'Well,' he said, 'you can pay for it or put it back.'

"So he put it back.

"When we got up in the woods, he told me to go down over the road and get his old cap.

"I said, 'I can't do it. The snow is deep.'

"Well, God, he took me and threw me down over the bank and I got his cap.

"I guess he learned it before he came to Tunbridge."

My mother made the suit I have on in the picture. She made all my clothes. I always thought a lot of my mother and dad.

That's my father's mother. She was a domestic nurse and took care of nearly one-hundred-fifty babies. Her husband died when she was forty eight. She was ninety three when she died and she was active right up till the last.

My grandfather on my mother's side, Charles Parker, was ninety-eight when he passed away. He never had a doctor in his life. He'd come up the Connecticut River from Connecticut somewhere in a canoe. He had just a few tools he'd made himself. He settled over in Brookfield. Bought a little piece of land and built a log cabin. Then he kept buying land and working for neighbors.

He built another house because he didn't have room in the log cabin for his first two children. I think he had seven children in all, including a son killed in the Civil War.

My mother said that when she was a girl at home she very seldom saw her father. He'd get up early in the morning, do his chores, eat his breakfast, grab his bag of crackers and cheese and jug of New England rum, and go to the woods. He told me the day he was ninety-five years old, he said, "Joe, I didn't have to go out and cut wood, but I wanted to show the young fellas what I could do. So I went out and cut a half a cord of wood and piled it up before dinner."

He was ninety eight when he died. I used to go into his room and visit with him. Of course, he had to clear all the land and he hewed the timber to build all the buildings. Them old-timers really had a rough time. But they enjoyed it. There warn't half so much sickness then as there is now.

He was five feet seven or eight. Good build. He had an axe, by gosh. He showed me the axe he always kept behind his bureau. He'd take that axe and shave the hair right off his wrist.

Some of the neighbors told me that after his son died in the Army he was never the same. They said that every year the second or third day of April he'd always go up over the hill down the rabbit tracks and shoot his musket off three times. He'd come back and clean it, put it up on the rack, and never touch it for another year. People didn't seem to know why, but that was about the time of year his son had died. He's buried down in Petersburg, Virginia.

I warn't very well in my younger days. Oh, I had a lot of stomach trouble. But I made it. I got married when I was eighteen; soon after that my father died. I used to enjoy helping him. A horse kicked him and stove his chest in and he got pneumonia. Of course, in them days they didn't know how to doctor pneumonia. He passed away in three days.

I hadn't been out of the Randolph Center agricultural school a year, but when my father died in 1916 I had to take over.

My dad and my grandfather always used to keep oxen. I used to raise em up and get the gain on em; I used to make a hundred dollars or more on em every year. I'd have em to work and then I'd sell em.

I bought my first pair of calves when I was ten years old. They

Joe Tuttle and his grandmother

were pretty near yearlings. I gave $45 for em, kept em a year, and sold em for $150.

I plowed a lot with oxen. Got wood and everything with em. I used to go and gather sap with oxen when I was a kid.

Of course, oxen have to be trained. Oh, it's quite a job sometimes to keep em in the furrow. Sometimes they get to crowding. There's two kinds of yokes, a straight yoke and a slide yoke. With a slide yoke, they can work back and forth.

I used to like to plow with oxen. I used to like to plow with horses. I liked horses better after I got grown up.

They wouldn't take me in World War I because my grandmother was old and my mother was along in years and wasn't too well. I was the only one on the farm. So they sent me home and told me to stay on the farm.

The high price of machinery and labor and taxes have hurt the farmer. Back in 1940 my taxes were $120. At the present time they run $2,000. We don't get any better service than we got for the $120.

I generally take a drink when I go to bed and sometimes when I get up in the morning. I have it right beside my bed. I just reach over and grab the bottle and take a drink. Half awake, I guess. It's kept me active so far.

After my first wife and I had been married a little while, I came home drunk and she said, "I ain't in favor of a man that drinks."

I said, "OK, by God, there's the road you came in on. Any time you're dissatisfied, take it out again."

And after that, never one word said.

She did tell me, "If you ever come home sober, I'll keel right over backwards on the floor."

I used to work down at the fairgrounds. Them horse fellows, you know, God, they liked cider and sap beer. I used to carry it down to em. God, they'd put the old liquor right to me.

If I warn't able to unhitch my horses off the wagon and hitch em onto the express wagon, they'd do it. And load me in. The old horses'd wake me up when they got home.

The first time I came home drunk was from helping to dedicate the Town Garage. Yeah, the liquor was flowing like water in the Town Garage. God, we used to have some high old times!

But sometimes it's been hard to make ends meet. But I kept agoin. I made money, but I had too many doctors' bills. My father and mother and my grandmother; I buried two wives. My son, he's been sick a lot.

Dr. Mitchell came to town when I was a small boy and he doctored here all his life. He used to tell me, "When I came to town, gosh," he says, "I didn't think you'd ever grow up to be a man. You were sickly. My God," he says, "I guess hard work made ya."

I've had three or four different old doctors tell me that they doctor more heart disease now in farmers than they used to when we done the hard work.

I like Dr. Martin. He has a nice personality. I was up there in Chelsea at his office and Doc introduced me to a new doctor. He says, "Give this man your recipe for living a long life."

I says, "I can't do it, Doc."

"Why not?"

I says, "I haven't lived only part of my life."

"Well," he says, "give me a recipe for living as long as ya have."

"Well, Doc, I always kept away from the women and I never used tobacca or likker."

He looked at me. "Joe," he says, "any bigger liars in Tunbridge than you are?" [*Laughter.*]

I says, "There might be, Doc."

Newton Washburn

BASKETMAKER

Bethlehem, New Hampshire
Born: 1915

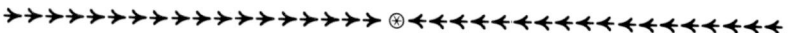

WOVEN BASKETS ARE ONE OF THOSE Indian legacies like snowshoes and maple sugar that give the north country its special character. Newton Washburn learned basketmaking from his mother, Lulu Sweetser Washburn, and from her large family in the Morrisville-Stowe-Waterbury area. (His mother was a sister of quiltmaker Belle Perry.) During the Depression, bushel baskets were the family's main source of livelihood, threatened temporarily by galvanized pails. "Then farmers found out that bushel baskets outwore the galvanized ones so they went back to baskets again."

In the early thirties, baskets were cheap, functional containers for vegetables, fruits, lard, laundry, and even the sawdust on which farmers bedded down their stock. Newton Washburn's family sold bushel baskets for a dollar and a quarter, poor pay for the slow work of turning a tree into woven masterpieces. For each bushel basket, he now earns seventy-five dollars from appreciative buyers, such as wool spinners. He also weaves laundry baskets and baby cradles on demand.

Washburn ash baskets are a pleasure to the eye and nose. They are very touchable. His baskets—with their star-shaped, raised bottoms; horizontal strips, called filling; vertical strips, called uprights; tops, or hooping; the binding strapped around the hooping, finished off with a carved, bent handle—all create a picture of elegant simplicity.

I was the only child. I guess I was about eight when I started making baskets by lamplight. Everyone in the family had to make em. I'm doing it the same now as I did then, only not by lamplight. [*Laughter.*]

My great-grandparents made baskets for their own use, like a lot of people did in those days. But my grandparents and parents made them for a living. In the winter they'd take their baskets to the store and trade em for groceries or whatever they needed. Because stores sold baskets. Same as a lot of times you'd take a bushel of potatoes down and trade em for something else you needed. Some different than it is now! [*Laughter.*]

Because my parents, grandparents, and great-grandparents were all basketmakers, I guess it came natural to me.

My mother had six sisters and six brothers and they were all basketmakers and all their children made baskets when they were children. Those children as they grew up got away from it. I'm the only basketmaker in the family left.

We were fortunate because my folks had a small farm. Most of the others rented small houses, but we had a farm. Everyone used to gather there in summer for a week or two to make baskets.

Most of em played some kind of an instrument and had beautiful singing voices. They'd make baskets all day, then drink a little homebrew and make a little music at night. It was a good life. Uncles, aunts, cousins.

Some made moonshine: white lightning. A lot of em made homebrew out of wheat. My dad always put ten or twelve barrels of cider down cellar cause we had about two hundred apple trees. So he had hard cider and they had homebrew and white lightning. They just had a good time.

They tell about the good old days. It was hard work, though. It wasn't like today. I would like to wake up tomorrow morning and see it back about 1930. I would! But what would the younger people do to make a living? They wouldn't know where to start. Today it takes a lot of money just to pay taxes. We had a 200-acre farm; our taxes were nineteen dollars a year.

My mother was a very fine basketmaker. My dad wasn't. She did such a unique job of it. Everything was so neatly done. Her baskets were all perfectly shaped. No sloppy work at all. She and one uncle were the two best basketmakers of them all.

Her maiden name was Lulu Sweetser and she had a heart of gold. She was everyone's friend; she'd help anyone she could. She was a beautiful singer and she played organ and piano. She was a lovely person.

Mother was strong. She weighed 220 pounds. It takes strength to go in the woods and get a log and pound the strips off. And to make the handles and the hooping you have to be strong in your hands to whittle them out and to bend em.

When the white people came here, the Indians were making

baskets with what they called basketwood. Now some people call basketwood brown ash and some call it black ash, but it is the same tree. In New Hampshire and upstate New York, they call it black ash. In Vermont most everyone calls it brown ash.

It's about the only wood you can pound off each year's growth. Farther south they do make baskets of white oak, but white oak doesn't grow here very abundantly and it doesn't make as good a basket. Brown ash will pick moisture out of the air and will always stay pliable; white oak will just keep getting drier and drier till it gets brittle and breaks.

You can find a lot of brown ash, but blight has gotten into many areas. On high land blight hasn't gotten to it. So I look on the mountains for all of my wood. I have eleven logs out here that loggers have brought to me. Enough for two or three years.

Brown ash grows only in wet areas so if you're back in the woods and find a wet place on the side of a mountain, like it might be a spring, that spot will be best. Bettern it is on the low land. Your growth rings don't get so thick on the mountain cause it grows slower and more evenly than down on the lowland.

You have to look for a good straight tree. One without any dead limbs. Because all you can take is the very best of it. Ordinarily one log out of the butt of the tree is all you can use. Eight foot is about as long as you can handle a log. So we cut em eight foot and if there's another four-foot piece, we take it to use for basket uprights.

You get a log, bring it home, peel the bark, and throw the bark away. The rest of the log you use. You beat the whole length of the log with a hammer to get strips off it. One year's growth to a time. Then you split it in whatever widths you're going to be using. To make it smooth you shave it on both sides with a knife and a leather on your leg. And go ahead and make your basket.

You have to leave about three inches at the core of the log. Sometimes if it's an exceptionally good log, you can split that up and use it for the hooping and the handles. So there's not much waste.

I make the bottom on this mold. It's a press to hold em in place cause there's from twenty-four to thirty-two pieces of material to weave. I put it on the press to lock it together till I get around four or five times. Then I take it in my lap and shape it. I don't use a mold after that.

You weave your bottom and get your uprights ready. You weave em wet. If the tree is green, no more than a couple of months old, you can do it without wetting. Of course, you have to keep a wet cover over the log.

You get the size bottom woven that you want and just bend your uprights up and hold it in your lap and just start weaving around it, keeping them upright. It's all done by eye. There are no forms or nothing.

In every basket, one upright has to be split because regardless of how many uprights you have, when you bend em up you're doubling the number. It always comes out an even number and you can't weave with an even number. So you have to split one to make an uneven number around so that it is a continuous weave. Otherwise, if you didn't split that upright, you'd have to weave around and lap it over and then start again; it wouldn't be a continuous weave basket.

The handle is a straight, narrow piece that's steamed and bent.

I think the difficult part on a large basket is getting the hooping out.

Younger people don't have the picture in their minds of what a basket should look like. So they use a mold. I don't.

There's a lot of workmen probably as good or better than I am, but my advantage is that I grew up with the baskets and know what they're supposed to look like. I know when they're right or not.

Lester Worthley

GENERAL STORE PROPRIETOR

East Corinth, Vermont
Born: 1889

COUNTRY STORES ARE ONE OF Vermont's most charming features. It's not so much what you can buy at them as the social contacts the stores foster. Especially those that are also post offices.

In his day Lester Worthley, now blind and almost a century old, was one of many storekeepers scattered throughout the state's villages. His shelves were stocked with hardware, tools, clothes, and food. There'd be cheese, lard, flour, corn meal, sugar, St. Johnsbury crackers, molasses, and vinegar. Lester would test the freshness of eggs that arrived in a packing of sawdust by holding them up to the light of a candle—a practice called candling. Like most storekeepers he worked very long hours—7 A.M. to 9 P.M. at the East Corinth store. For his pains he was very pleased if he took in forty dollars a day.

He was also postmaster for forty-two years.

Lester Worthley's business was geared to his villagers and farmers, almost a captive clientele, because until paved roads were built people shopped where they lived. The odd thing about this from the 1980s point of view is that none of his customers were tourists.

Lester did his courting in a horse and buggy. He went with his wife Susan for seven years before they married, the same year he bought the store. They lived in an apartment upstairs, initially with kerosene lamps and outdoor facilities. She used to clerk in the store, too, and might easily go from reaching into a barrel of brine to get someone a piece of salt pork to measuring a yard of lace. Their storekeeper's lot was an all-consuming one.

Lester told me that in his early days women's stocking had all been black. His wife Susan said once, "We thought we had quite an up to-date-store when we got brown stockings."

The thing that never goes out of date about the country store is its people.

I think that coming to my store was something people looked forward to. In those days there was no other place to go. So men sat around the back end of the store in the evening. Not every single night, but all times of the year. 'Cause in those days people didn't have automobiles.

There were most always one or two benches and extra chairs. Some would come in and sit down on the floor, stick their legs out, and talk, and chew the rag, and visit and smoke. And chew probably. [*Laughter.*] There was always a spittoon there for spitters. They'd talk about the people in the village and whatever activity there was. People often got their lanterns mixed up outside, which gave them an excuse to come back the next night to gather around the stove again.

Customers were the people that lived in East Corinth village and out on the farms. They dressed in their everyday farm clothes. In the daytime the farmers used to come to town to the creamery with their horse and express wagons. In the evening people came mostly on foot. Some would hitch up their buggy rig and drive to the store, not so much to sit around the store and gossip as they did to trade, to buy what they needed. People came in the evening mostly to visit and talk about the neighbors. [*Laughter.*] That's what they came for. To sit around and talk about what was going on. And talk about the other fella.

Politics. Oh, they talked about everything. There wasn't anything that they left out.

It was a social center. Especially for the women shoppers. The women would go to the store to shop and trade perhaps more than the men did. And people came into the post office every day to get their mail.

Those old-timers shopped differently. They'd take their eggs and butter and sometimes potatoes and sell them to the store where they bought their goods. The old-time stores used to swap. Most everybody had a few hens in those days and the store was their outlet for the eggs.

I can remember that I used to have any quantity of people that I could call *my* customers. My store was the only place they ever went. Now a storekeeper don't have "my customer"; everybody goes everywhere to trade nowadays.

The clerk waited on the customer in those days. Today when anybody goes to the store he has to wait on himself.

I sold cheese the same as every country store did, a big wheel about a foot and a half across. It was made right here in Vermont at Cabot. And do you know what a St. Johnsbury cracker used to look like? It's a cracker they used to eat with milk. Two pieces put together. You'd sell em out by the pound, but they also had the same kind packed up in cartons.

When they first started selling raisins in packages, a woman came into the store one morning and she asked me if I'd take half a dozen raisins out of the package and give em to her 'cause she didn't want to buy a whole package of raisins. I didn't accommodate the lady. She was too thrifty! I was always honest. I wouldn't take a half dozen raisins out of a package and then sell the package to somebody else. Of course not!

Most every young boy ten years old has something he aims for. And I thought I wanted to run a country store.

Why, you might consider me one of the prominent citizens of the village. I never was mayor but I was somewhat connected with everything that went on. I used to know everybody in town and how many children they had, what the children's names were, what their ages were, and all about it. [*Laughter.*] I liked it.

Becky Bangs

ADVENTURER AND CROSS-COUNTRY SKIER

Newark, Vermont
Born: 1958

Herman "Jackrabbit" Johannsen

ADVENTURER AND CROSS-COUNTRY SKIER

Piedmont, Quebec
Born: 1875

➤➤➤➤➤➤➤➤➤➤➤➤➤➤➤ ⊗ ◄◄◄◄◄◄◄◄◄◄◄◄◄◄◄◄◄

TWENTY-SIX-YEAR-OLD BECKY BANGS and I drove up to Montreal from the Northeast Kingdom in a snowstorm to find her hero, one-hundred-and-ten-year-old Jackrabbit Johannsen. We were directed down a long corridor in a church-run retirement home. Along the way we passed two old ladies who were talking excitedly beside a window. "He's out there again today," said one seventy-ish grandma to another.

We found Jackrabbit out in the snow, waving a pair of ski poles around his head and breathing deeply the fresh, cold air. The scene was too good to be true: the frail seniors huddled inside the overheated building and the legendary wilderness skier outside enjoying the storm.

He was about forty years older than they were, but he had skied well into his nineties before his knees finally gave out. When Becky offered him her arm for a walk along the snowy path, an electric glow of youth suffused his face.

Becky Bangs had long wanted to meet her hero, the man considered to be the father of North American ski touring. Like Jackrabbit, she is an adventurer. She has bicycled three times across Europe and once across the United States. A sailing trip from Mexico to the South Seas ended in a mutiny in the Cook Islands "because the skipper went crazy and our lives were threatened." Most important for our meeting with the old Norwegian, she had skied competitively for the Williams College cross-country team.

Our conversation in Jackrabbit's spartan room was to touch on many subjects, from marriage to dog teams. What we carried away most from the meeting was this man's enthusiasm. We had the feeling that we were experiencing a phenomenon. From his strong handshake to the twinkle in his eye, Jackrabbit Johannsen was all go. He showed us his honorary ski bib from the more than four thousand-person marathon he had attended the weekend before. And he forcefully explained his plan to rally the building's old people to exchange their sedentary habits for exercise and fitness. "I'm forcing the elderly people into doing something. They don't live in the right way so how can they expect to continue living? If they close up everything in winter and don't go out?"

Of course, Jackrabbit is unusual because he has lived well past the century mark. But it is not age alone that excites the admiration of his many fans throughout the North. The facts about his life are simple: He was born in Norway June 15, 1875; attended military academy there; studied engineering in Berlin; and emigrated to Ohio in 1894 to sell heavy equipment all over North America from the Panama Canal to the Arctic. "It was adventure I wanted," he says. "I wasn't so much interested in the engineering as I was in getting adventure. In seeing something new and learning new lands."

He thanks wilderness for his pleasure and success in life. In 1902 his company sent him to Quebec where the railway was under construction north of North Bay. There, Herman Johannsen lived with the Cree Indians and earned the name Chief Jackrabbit by persuading them to use skis when trapping instead of snowshoes. Later he created the Maple Leaf Trail and introduced several generations of Canadians and Americans to the joys of cross-country, especially wilderness ski touring. "The people who live in town are not interested in sports for themselves," he says. "They just want to see it on television. So we are trying to get them used to wilderness and to what God has to offer in nature."

Stories about Jackrabbit are legion. My favorite has him landing a canoe party on a remote lakeshore, where he was challenged by the Cree guide of another group already camped there. Jackrabbit not only gave the man a lecture on wilderness hospitality but also told him that his father, whom Jackrabbit had known years earlier, would be ashamed of his selfishness. All this in the Cree language. The Indian guide was openmouthed in astonishment and quickly made amends.

As remarkable as Jackrabbit's enthusiasm and age is his dedication to wilderness adventure, something he shared with his generation of Norwegian explorers. I wanted to see how a Vermont youngster would react to such a hero. Many pundits today say that the hero is as obsolete as the horse and buggy and that we were born too late to do great deeds. This book has been my counterargument. I want to leave you with the thoughts of both my oldest hero, Jackrabbit Johannsen, and my youngest, Becky Bangs.

HERMAN "JACKRABBIT" JOHANNSEN

I was born and got used to the wilderness in Norway, where we led a natural life. Later that came in handy because it made me feel at home in the Canadian wilderness. In 1930 we got into the bad Depression—I had started in business for myself—and I lost everything. But I didn't go back to business. From 1930 on I lived in the wilderness. I lived off the land: fishing, hunting, and skiing, and really had a wonderful life.

And I got that due to having heroes like Fridtjof Nansen. He went across Greenland in 1888 on skis. That was the first crossing of the inland ice in Greenland. When he came back, then they found out in Europe and England what skis were. That trip across Greenland made skis known in Europe and in the other parts of the world.

Nansen had been just an ordinary boy in school, but he became known because he did something. He crossed Greenland. He had a trip to get to the North Pole with another fellow. Their expedition drifted in a sailing vessel frozen in the north polar ice. When they got as close to the pole as they thought they could get, the two of them left by sledge. They were gone for fifteen months in the

Becky Bangs and Herman "Jackrabbit" Johannsen

open in the Arctic until they finally got back to Franz Josef Land.

Nansen was a wonderful fellow. I knew him very well. As a matter of fact, his eldest daughter married a cousin of mine.

He had a great influence on us younger fellows. (I was ten years younger.) And he had us running from ice floe to ice floe, jumping from floe to floe. Oh, wonderful! Well, he was a great man. That's a hero!

Amundsen was a schoolmate of mine—just an ordinary boy in school. He was not a good competitive skier. I was in competition. I remember one winter trip I had with him in 1893. He was a plugger and systematic. Then he got used to handling dogs and dog sleds and to living in the Arctic. He gradually built up and was the first to sail the Northwest Passage. Later he took the *Fram*, Nansen's old ship, to the South Pole.

I knew Otto Sverdrup very well, too. He was with Nansen on Greenland in 1888. He was with Nansen on the first North Pole expedition when as captain of the *Fram* he drifted across the Arctic Ocean. He took the *Fram* on another expedition in 1898; I came very near to going on that myself. I was just about to sign up when my father found some money so I could continue my study as an engineer. Eventually I came to Canada anyway.

Nobody leaves Norway because he doesn't like it. He leaves Norway in order to see what the rest of the world is like. I was out from the very start in my life after adventure. And I always had skis with me ever since I first left Norway.

Today the people who cross-country ski want the track made for them. You shouldn't have any track. You should make the track yourself. You should ski in any kind of country or conditions. And make the skis what they are supposed to be: a means of transportation, a means of going from one place to another. Today everybody wants to make money on it.

There's too darned much monkeybusiness. Too much of this artificial stuff. Get back to nature. Live in the right way. Smoke a pipe and take a drink in moderation. Take advantage of all the good things in life the proper way. Live in the right way. Skiing is a sport, not a business. Skiing is a sport that should be used by everybody who is fortunate enough to live in a ski country.

I remember a camp where they were interested in canoeing and in skiing. They used to say, "Rise before dawn, free of care. Seek adventure. Let noon find you on some other lake and night overtake you anywhere at home." That's the spirit!

Take the province of Quebec. Wonderful country! In winter you can go on skis over the same portages, the height of land, where you traveled with a canoe in summer. February, March, and April are the best time of the year in Canada and in the northern United States. You can make a long distance traveling over the hard snow on portages from campsite to campsite. As you travel through the bush, you can see the life of the animals on the portages. Moose, deer, wolf, fox—it's the mating season of the fox and the wolf. All the time you can see the animals and their tracks in the snow. The country is alive!

You start in the morning at 30 or 40 degrees below zero. Get out of your sleeping bag, take a snow bath by the fire where the embers are still glowing. Then pack up and go. Start the next campsite at noon. Get the wood together. Build a big fire that'll last you all night. That's the way to live. I have done a lot of that.

A tent is all right when there's a thaw. Then you get wet if you sleep in the snow. But if you have a good sleeping bag with a reindeer or caribou skin inside and a waterproof cover on the outside, you bed down in the snow. If it's cold enough, you're all right. You sleep well. You wake up in the morning ready for adventure.

That's the life!

BECKY BANGS

I don't know when I first heard about Jackrabbit because he is a legend that cross-country skiers grow up with. I didn't know a lot about him, but I did know that he was an old man who brought cross-country skiing to this country.

In my family, we started skiing as soon as we could walk. I did some alpine racing and didn't like racing through the gates as fast as I could. When I was eight, we all got cross-country skis for Christmas. Somebody took us out and gave us a lesson about half an hour before we raced in our first race. There were fourteen people in the race. Boys and girls of all ages mixed together because there weren't many people racing cross-country back then. I stuck with it and, as the sport grew, I went with it. I raced all the way through college, until I decided that I'd had it with competition. Now I just like to get out and get some exercise and enjoy nature.

Sometimes when you think about a person a lot, he doesn't meet those expectations. But Jackrabbit met them and then some. When we went out in the snow and asked him if he wanted to go for a walk and he tried to jump up and I saw the enthusiasm that he had—it was more than I had expected. The way he looked was really perfect, too. He had on the same hat and the same sweater as in the pictures I'd seen.

About ten years ago, Jackrabbit came to Lyndonville. There was a picture of him on the front page of the newspaper wearing a blue and white Norwegian sweater. Since that time I wanted one like that. For my birthday last year my mother bought me the yarn and the pattern. I finished it about four months ago. I wore it when we went to see him. When he took his coat off and he was wearing the same sweater, I was pretty happy.

I remember his appreciation of the simple life and of nature and of how we should enjoy that above all else.

What also struck me was that he emphasized that the explorers he chose as his heroes were just ordinary people — schoolboy friends of his — who went out and took advantage of what was given to them. They didn't sit at home. They went out after things. I think that's very important.

I've done a few things. In doing them I learned that there is so much more out there to do.

I consider a hero to be someone who inspires you. Someone to whom you look for guidance. And although I'm not one to go camp out overnight when it's forty below and then take a snow bath, I do think that living a life of, oh, I hate to say risk, but going out and doing the exciting things is something that makes life worthwhile.

He has done that. He's an inspiration to continue going out and walking on the wild side.

Glossary

➤➤➤➤➤➤➤➤➤➤➤➤➤➤➤➤➤➤ ✳ ◄◄◄◄◄◄ ◄◄◄◄◄◄◄◄◄◄◄◄◄◄◄

Arch. A bricked-up firebox that slants up from the firegrates beneath a maple syrup evaporator.

Barway. An opening of removable poles through a fence or hedgerow.

Bend, the. Greensboro Bend in Orleans County.

Stone boat. A flat plank sled used by farmers for removing stones from fields and by horse pulling contestants for pulling measured weights. The team's harness is attached to a board at the front of the boat. (The "board" is a large steel plate with a curved, raised front.)

Bridle chains (sled runner chains). Chains that are looped around the runners of a sled to slow its downhill progress.

Dooryard. That part of a yard immediately outside the most used entrance of a house.

Dray. A horsedrawn vehicle with sled runners in front and two pivoting intersecting poles dragging behind. Drays are used for carrying pulpwood, firewood, sugar buckets, and so on.

Going flat out. Working very hard.

Governor, the. George Aiken.

Hames. Two curved pieces of iron or wood on the horse collar to which traces are attached.

Heavey. As in a horse which has the heaves, a respiratory ailment usually caused by dust.

Hitchers. The men who attach a team to a loaded boat in a horse pulling contest.

Johnnycake. Corn bread baked in a big pan and cut into squares.

Lister. A tax appraiser who prepares the grand list of locally taxable property.

Rails. Two boundary lines made of wood which a team of pulling horses must stay between when pulling their loaded boat the required distance.

Road commissioner. The elected town official who is in charge of keeping the roads in good condition.

Rowen. A season's second cutting of hay.

Selectman. The three selectmen are a town's chief elected officials and are elected at the annual town meeting.

Spreaders. Loops extending from the hames through which the reins can be passed.

St. Johnsbury cracker. A hard, plain soda cracker that easily breaks in two and is eaten with coffee, milk, or soup.

Sugarbush. The woodlot of maple trees from which a farmer gathers his sap.

32 class. A weight category for a team of pulling horses, representing a total weight of 3,200 pounds.

Tip-up. A small flag activated when a baited hook beneath the ice catches a fish.

Town Farm. Formerly a farm operated by a town as a home for the indigent.

Tug. The leather or chain strap or trace between the horse collar and the whippletree at the front of the vehicle.

Ville, the. Lyndonville in Caledonia County.

Warning. A list of issues, including revenue and tax measures, to be discussed at town meeting. The selectmen usually publish the warning in the form of a little booklet. The material is primarily local, though a few statewide and national issues are sometimes included.

Whippletree (or whiffletree or singletree). A pivoted crossbar with metal hardware that attaches the vehicle to the tugs or traces pulling it. The two-horse team would have doubletrees or "eveners" instead.

Index

➤➤➤➤➤➤➤➤➤➤➤➤➤➤➤➤➤➤➤ ✳ ◄◄◄◄◄◄◄◄◄◄◄◄◄◄◄◄◄◄◄◄◄